The
WISDOM of the
VEDAS

The
WISDOM of the
VEDAS

J.C. Chatterji

A publication supported by
THE KERN FOUNDATION

Quest Books
Theosophical Publishing House

Wheaton, Illinois ♦ Chennai (Madras), India

First Quest Edition 1980
Revised Edition 1992
Sixth Printing 2008

Quest Books
The Theosophical Publishing House
P.O. Box 270
Wheaton, IL 60189-0270

www.questbooks.net

Library of Congress Cataloging-in-Publication Data

Chatterji, Jagadish Chandra.
The wisdom of the Vedas / J. C. Chatterji.
    p.   cm. (Theosophical Heritage Classics)
ISBN 978-0-8356-0684-4
1. Vedas—Criticism, interpretation, etc.   I. Title.
BL1112.26 C47 1992
294.5'921—dc20   92-50142
                                                    CIP

Printed in the United States of America

Contents

Publisher's Note

The Wisdom of the Vedas was first published in 1931 by Kailas Press under the title *India's Outlook on Life*. The second edition, under the present title, was published by Theosophical Publishing House in 1973, and came out under the Quest imprint in 1980.

The present edition has been edited to reflect the modern use of inclusive language. *He* and *him* referring to a human being have been changed, usually to the plural. It was more problematic to find pronouns that refer to the different names of the Divine. Chatterji says (note 7), "It is absurd to refer to Brahman, the all-intelligent, all-bliss, and ever-abiding Being, by the pronoun *it*." Brahman is neither male nor female, but "certainly not an unintelligent neuter entity such as a stone." In this edition we have elected to refer to Brahman and Atman as *THAT* or *That One* rather than *he* or *him*, which appeared in the original. *Purusha* is sometimes translated as *The Person* and is associated with masculinity in Sanskrit. Therefore, we kept the masculine pronouns that refer to Purusha.

We have added subheadings for readability. In other minor changes, we have broken down overly long sentences and paragraphs, occasionally smoothed out an unclear or awkward expression, and eliminated diacritical marks. Though these marks help in pronouncing Sanskrit words, we feel that they are a hindrance to most of our readers, who do not know Sanskrit. We have also qualified references to ether, a concept no longer in good standing in science.

In this edition we have included an introduction by David Frawley, Vedic scholar and author of such books as *Gods, Sages and Kings: Vedic Secrets of Ancient Civilization* (Passage Press, 1991) and *From the River of Heaven: Hindu and Vedic Knowledge for the Modern Age* (Passage Press, 1990). This introduction reflects the current state of Vedic research. In addition to John Dewey's original foreword, we have included a piece by Kurt F. Leidecker, Professor Emeritus, Asian Studies, Mary Washington College, which originally appeared as a review in *Main Currents in Modern Thought* (Nov.-Dec. 1973). This piece has been slightly edited to make it suitable for a foreword.

The book was originally dedicated to "the friends of India in America" and was offered as a contribution to that great bridge of friendship between East and West which can come only from a deeper mutual understanding of the two approaches to life. This lucid statement of Indian philosophy seems even more useful now that so much of Eastern thought and philosophy has come to the West.

Preface

The present exposition of India's outlook on life, which is based ultimately on the Veda, has been prepared in response to repeated requests for a concise and comprehensive statement as to how the Veda, the most ancient wisdom of India, regards life, its origin, purpose, and goal. The writer knows of no other publication which covers this entire ground in so short a compass. It is believed, therefore, that the following presentation of the subject will prove serviceable not only as an introduction to a deeper and wider study, but also as a convenient summary of the salient points.

Ancient as it is, this view of life, when properly understood in all of its implications, may very well throw a flood of light on many an unsolved problem—philosophic, ethical, religious, social, and even scientific—of these our modern times.

Professor E. Washburn Hopkins and Professor S. Radhakrishnan have kindly glanced through these pages in proof and sent the author appreciative comments.

It is a great pleasure to acknowledge with

Preface

gratitude the courtesy and kindness of Professor Dewey, of Columbia University, who, despite the pressure of multifarious duties, not only found time to examine the work with care, but also very graciously consented to write the Foreword to the First Edition of this little volume.

JAGADISH CHANDRA CHATTERJI

NEW YORK
JANUARY 14, 1931

Foreword to the First Edition

John Dewey

It would be difficult to find one less fitted by previous study and knowledge to write an introduction to an account of Vedic philosophy than the present writer. But, with the increasing intellectual contact of the East and West, it is obviously of importance that we of the Western world should have authentic information regarding the culture of India. The philosophy associated with Brahmanism is an essential part of that culture. In some respects knowledge of it is a key to the historic thought of India. Not only all scholars, therefore, but all interested in promoting spiritual exchange between the East and the West will welcome the series of publications of which this is the initial number.

Even one who, like myself, is not expert in Vedic philosophy will recognize the system, thoroughness, and lucidity with which Pandit Chatterji has presented that philosophy. It may safely be said that nowhere will the reader and student find available such a comprehensive and clear account set forth by a competent authority. It is not necessary to say to the Western reader that the foundations and the method of this Oriental system of thought are far removed from those current with us; it is not easy to translate from one system into the other. This very fact increases the value of the complete and clear statement which is set before us. It gives a much needed chart of bearings.

COLUMBIA UNIVERSITY
MAY 5, 1930

Foreword to the Third Edition

Kurt F. Leidecker

The Wisdom of the Vedas is a small but highly significant book by one of India's great Sanskrit pandits of the old school, who earned for himself the degree of Vidya-varidhi ("Ocean of Learning").

Early in this century, the author, a B. A. *Cantab.*, was Director of the Archaeological and Research Department of Kashmir State, and in that capacity edited the highly important *Kashmir Series of Texts and Studies*, brought out at Srinagar, India, in Sanskrit with scholarly apparatus and on excellent paper, a rarity in India at that time. It was through these texts that Western scholars became acquainted with the Advaita Shaiva System of Kashmir, which has now to be added to the other great systems of Indian philosophy. Pandit Chatterji also published *Kashmir Shaivism* (second in the series alluded to, now published by State University of New York Press) and *Hindu Realism* (Allahabad, 1912), which should be read after this introductory volume.

What distinguishes this book on India's

outlook on life is its originality. In method it does not follow the traditional presentations of Western writers from Max Müller onward. It is an exposition, not of *one* of India's philosophies, but of India's *philosophy,* and is distinguished in that it anticipates some modern thinking about the cosmos as well as on psychology and metaphysics. It takes into account the basic etymologies of Sanskrit words and symbolisms, both approaches that are proving highly useful in the interpretation of Vedic literature, other methods having failed us.

The forte of the author is his lucid English and familiarity with Western philosophy. He makes no compromises, but highlights the points of contact which may be pursued for better East-West understanding. Sarvevalli Radhakrishnan, the doyen of Indian philosophy, called this volume of Pandit Chatterji's "an authentic guide to the study of the central features of the Vedic philosophy"; E. Washburn Hopkins, the American Sanskritist, suggested that through Chatterji's treatment India's outlook "may in essentials" be what "modern scientific thought is almost prepared to adopt"; John Dewey, not known to be in favor of any idealism, called it "a much needed chart of bearings."

The present edition lacks some of the

diacritical marks which help in making Sanskrit words more correctly pronounceable. But the usefulness and importance of the book far outweigh these technical trivia in the present edition. Whatever motives prompt students of Indian thought, they all should acquire *The Wisdom of the Vedas*. For nowhere will they find such a condensation of the essentials of Indian philosophy. Let them not be misled by "Vedas" in the title—a term which is used quite restrictedly by Western scholarship. *Veda* means *wisdom* or *science* which, in the words of the author, is based on "Mantras, which are the primary compositions" of the oldest Indian literature, and "Brahmanas, which are a sort of illustrative commentary on the Mantras."

What this book sets forth is, thus, how humans may achieve ultimate freedom and the consummation of life according to the greatest of India's minds, reaching back into the dim past. But withal, Pandit Chatterji's objective was to foster universal understanding. It was his dream to develop the International School of Vedic and Allied Research with branches in New York, London, Banares and Srinagar, a project in which this reviewer was intimately involved. The great American depression of the thirties put an end to this dream. Let us hope that through this edition of one of Pandit Chatterji's works, new interest will be stimulated in the age-old quest for life's meaning.

MARY WASHINGTON COLLEGE
NOVEMBER, 1973

Introduction: Some Background

David Frawley

The Vedas are the original scripture or source teaching of the Hindu tradition, from which its many branches of Vedanta, Yoga, and Tantra have emerged through time, and to which they all look back with reverence. Hence a study of the Vedas is essential for all those who wish to understand the foundation of these different teachings. The Vedas, moreover, are the background relative to which the Buddhist religion evolved, and Buddhism also preserves many Vedic terms and practices. Hence a study of the Vedas is also important for understanding the Buddhist traditions of the Far East.

Moreover, the Vedas are the oldest known Indo-European religious and philosophical tradition, antedating that of the Greeks by some centuries. A study of the Vedas is therefore relevant for discovering the original spiritual impulses behind all Indo-European traditions. Thus an examination of the Vedas remains central for anyone interested in the deeper spiritual inquiries of the human race.

1

Introduction

Historians have previously dated the Vedas from 1500-500 BC, making them the largest mass of ancient literature that we possess. However, recent archaeological research in India suggests that the Vedas are much older than this. A large ancient urban civilization was discovered in India in the early part of this century, called the "Indus Valley" culture after the region in which its initial sites were located, or "Harappa and Mohenjodaro" after its two major cities. Dated from 2700-1900 BC, it covered western India and Pakistan with sites into Central Asia. Originally it was thought to be pre-Vedic or non-Indo-European, but it is now being reinterpreted as an Indo-European and Vedic culture.

The great river of India spoken of in the Vedas—the Sarasvati—has recently been rediscovered and appears to have been the central homeland of the Indus Valley culture. This river, which flowed southwest in the region west of modern Delhi, roughly paralleling the Indus to the sea, contains hundreds of Indus culture sites positioned all along its dried banks. The Indus civilization, now renamed by many the "Sarasvati civilization," came to an end with the drying up of the river around 1900 BC. As the Vedas speak of the Sarasvati River as having a wide course from the mountains to the sea, they must date from the period while the river was still flowing and must reflect the civilization located on it. This dates the Vedas well before 2000 BC, and makes them the oldest continuous religious and philosophical tradition in the world, contemporary with the pyramids of Egypt.

This new information on the Vedas should again bring our attention back to these ancient wisdom books of humanity, which makes the republication of this classic on the Vedas by Pandit Chatterji welcome again.

The Vedas are said to represent the perennial philosophy and to be a manifestation of Sanatana Dharma, which literally means the eternal truth. The Vedic approach is thus universal—an attempt to direct us toward the solution of the ultimate truths that any serious thinking person must examine. Hence the Vedas do not set forth any dogma, nor insist that we believe in anything in particular. They are not focused on a particular teacher or prophet, a specific revelation, or historical event. Rather they make the individual, we ourselves, important, as truth, according to the Vedic perspective, is something that we must discover for ourselves. The Vedas ask us only to have an open mind and a serious approach and to examine impersonally the contents of our own consciousness. The Vedic

concern is to help us understand our own
nature and the truth of the mysterious universe
in which we live. For this, the Vedas set forth
certain lines of inquiry that remain relevant
even in the modern world.

The Vedas are concerned with the ultimate
questions of human life: Who are we? Why
were we born? And what in us, if anything,
transcends death? The Vedas ask these
questions and show how various great sages
and yogis were able to answer them, not
merely theoretically, but by arriving at a
higher consciousness that transcends all
dilemma and doubt. The ultimate concern of
the Vedas is thus very practical: Why do we
suffer? By knowing that can we transcend
all pain?

The Vedas examine the nature of the
universe in which we live in the same manner
—not as an object to be dissected externally
but as a reality to be communed with in
consciousness. They ask: What is the ultimate
principle of this vast universe and how does
it relate to our own being? The conclusion
of Vedic inquiry is that there exists within
us an immortal and eternal being which is
the same as the immortal and eternal being
that pervades the entire universe, by knowing
which we transcend all death and sorrow. Our
Atman or inner Self is one with the Brahman

or supreme and infinite principle behind all the objects in the world. This is the same conclusion that all the great mystics of the world reach, though in the Vedas this approach is clear and examined from many angles.

Yet the Vedas do not merely ask us to accept such conclusions. They even tell us that it is better to doubt them until we ourselves actually find them to be true. Rather the Vedas present their teachings as models of lines of examination for us to adapt into the circumstances of our own lives.

The Vedic approach, therefore, is not merely a way of discursive or dialectical thinking but a way of meditation. The Vedas show the experience of great souls who searched out and discovered the ultimate meaning of existence. The Vedas thus relate to the practice of yoga or various spiritual practices designed to develop the mind to the point that it can comprehend such higher realities.

Vedic thought has already had its imprint on such important Western thinkers as Emerson, Thoreau, Whitman, and Schopenhauer. In recent years the influence of Vedic thought, largely through different yoga systems that have come to the West, has increased significantly. However, many yoga students have not examined the basic Vedic source teachings from which their traditions arise, an opportunity which this book affords. The very freedom and objectivity of the Vedic approach strikes a kindred chord in free thinkers today who are also sensitive to the sacred nature of the universe.

The present volume of Pandit Chatterji relates the essence of Vedic wisdom, as set forth in the Upanishads. This essence of Vedic knowledge is also called Vedanta, or the end of the Vedas, as it represents the culminating insights of Vedic thought. Hence this book can also be examined as a primary treatise on Vedanta and is one of the most important recent studies relative to it. The book relates to the higher or philosophical portion of Vedic inquiry, rather than to the ritualistic or cultural aspects, which are not of such importance. In this regard, the author mainly follows the Advaita Vedanta system of the philosopher-sage Shankaracharya.

The Wisdom of the Vedas sets forth Vedic knowledge in clear, scientific and modern terms, with lucid explanations, thus making it accessible to those of a Western background who may find such mystical or oriental ideas to be hard to grasp. The author explains the Vedic view both of the universe and of the human being, and sets forth the Vedic formulation of the universal principles that govern both the mind and the cosmos as a single, integral reality. The Vedas show the individual human being as containing the entire universe in his or her deepest consciousness. As such they can help us overcome the present alienation that we feel in our relationship to the world around us.

Specifically the author goes into detail in regard to the functions of the mind, thus revealing layers of consciousness and insight that are part of our deeper nature, beyond what is ordinarily accessible to us. Such information is useful for studying any depth psychology or for any meditation approach.

This book has long been considered one of the most important modern presentations of Vedic knowledge and is likely to remain so for some time to come. It provides readers a living sense of Vedic wisdom that is likely to change their lives if they ponder on it deeply. To look at the Vedas with an open mind and heart is to rediscover one's deeper being that appeared to be lost in the waves of time and circumstance.

SANTA FE, NEW MEXICO
MARCH, 1992

Parvati. Bronze (Width 38.7 cm, diameter 29 cm, height 95.2 cm.) India, Tamil Nadu. 16th Century, Vijayanagar.
Kate S. Buckingham Collection, 1961.776.

Part I

We sit as in a boundless Phantasmagoria and Dream-grotto; boundless, for the faintest star, the remotest century, lies not even nearer the verge thereof: sounds and many-coloured visions flit around our sense; but Him, the Unslumbering, whose work both Dream and Dreamer are, we see not; except in rare half-waking moments, suspect not. . . . Then, in that strange Dream, how we clutch at shadows as if they were substances; and sleep deepest while fancying ourselves most awake! . . . This Dreaming, this Somnambulism is what we on earth call Life; wherein the most indeed undoubtingly wander. . . .

Nevertheless, has not a deeper meditation taught certain of every climate and age, that the WHERE and WHEN, so mysteriously inseparable from all our thoughts, are but superficial terrestrial adhesions to thought; that the Seer may discern them where they mount up out of the celestial EVERYWHERE and FOREVER: have not all nations conceived their God as Omnipresent and Eternal; as existing in a universal HERE, and everlasting NOW? Think well, thou too wilt find that Space is but a mode of our human Sense, so likewise Time; there is no Space and no Time: WE are — we know not what; — light-sparkles floating in the aether of Deity!

So that this so solid-seeming World, after all, were but an air-image, our ME the only reality: and Nature, with its thousandfold production and destruction, but the reflex of our own inward Force, the "phantasy of our Dream."

THOMAS CARLYLE, **Sartor Resartus,**
BOOK I, CHAPTER VIII

Part I

The name *Veda* (or, as in the plural, Vedas) literally means Wisdom or Science, but is given, technically, to the oldest literature of the Indian people. This literature, going back to thousands of years before the beginning of the Christian era, consists traditionally of two definite groups, known as Mantras, which are the primary compositions, and Brahmanas, which are a sort of illustrative commentary on the Mantras. In the following pages, too, the name will be used in the same traditional sense, meaning the whole collection of both the Mantras and the Brahmanas, and therefore including, of course, the famous ten or twelve Upanishads.

Neither in the Mantra nor in the Brahmana portion are the Vedas a systematic treatise on the Vedic view of life that is to be presented here. Yet all the elements of this view are to be found scattered in the different parts of the Vedic literature and have been gathered together and treated systematically by various writers from very early times.[1] What is to follow here is a similar, though very brief, treatment of the Vedic material on the subject.

This treatment follows, moreover, the general traditional understanding of the matter, but in a manner which is intended to facilitate its comprehension by those not specially acquainted with the ancient way of viewing life. The Vedic view of life, then, both as reflected in the literature of the Vedas and as followed in India to this day, may be summarized as follows:

There is nothing absolutely stable, nothing permanently abiding, in the whole of the objective universe, which is but a system of ceaseless "goings on" (*jagati*, collective movement) with everything in it continually moving and changing (*jagat*).

This ceaseless movement in the universe, however, is not merely a mad dance; there is method in it and the movements are arranged in groups and "made to dwell" (*avasya*) within limits and for periods of various lengths, so as to give them what looks like stability, more or less enduring.[2]

What gives the systems of movements this apparent stability, orderly arrangement, and regulated sequence is not any property of the movements themselves, but is something other than the movements, being a power that rules them (*ish*) and "makes them dwell diversely" and in order.

The exact nature of this power, whether

feeling or unfeeling, conscious or unconscious, intelligent or unintelligent, whether absolutely stable and abiding or only apparently so—all this cannot possibly be definitely known nor can the power be directly contacted by way of the movements. Indeed, the movements themselves are cognized not directly but only inferentially as the cause of the sensations which alone are experienced directly and intimately. The power ruling the movements is thus doubly and impenetrably veiled from us by the sensations directly experienced and by the movements inferred as the sources of the sensations.

A Direct Approach

But while our entrance to the core of things by way of the senses is thus effectually barred, there is nevertheless a gateway of direct approach to what lies beyond the veil of sense perceptions and even beyond the movements, and, standing there, imparts that apparent stability and order which we experience in regard to the ever-fleeting show of the objective universe. This gateway of entering directly into the heart of things is, however, one which can be discovered only if we turn our attention away from the objective universe and dive down deep into what constitutes the subjective nature of every one of us as an individual. "Nowhere else is there a way of reaching" the heart of the universe.[3]

It is true that, in regard to what we are as individuals subjectively, equally as in the objective sphere, all is movement. We find that our bodies as well as our thoughts, feelings, ideas, and all mental states, i.e., all that conglomerate vaguely called the mind or soul— all these are continually moving and changing; in all of them there is nothing whatsoever that is absolutely stable and permanent.

Still we have a feeling—an illusory feeling, no doubt—that even though we, as individuals, be only ever-shifting aggregates of "mental states" and "complexes" and equally ever-changing aggregates of bodily cells, we are yet somehow stable and abiding entities, so that every one of us has the experience: "I am one and the same person yesterday, today, and the day after—the same John Smith from childhood to death." And illusory as is the feeling of stability and continuity in regard to the ever-changing complex of an individual ego or soul, this illusion, like all others, must have a basis in fact and in an actual experience of the fact. This fact is to be found in the presence —as the ground of our existence, and back of all mental states and all physical aggregates, and, as it were, wrapped up in them as in so many coatings (*kosha*)—of an entity that does not change, and is, therefore, a timeless Being (*sat*). And we have the direct experience, however vague, of this Being in the uttermost depths of our existence: we feel that we *are*. In the Vedic language, this Being, in the aspect that constitutes the ultimate Self and ground of our existence, is called *Atman*; but in translating Atman, as used in this connection, by "Self" one has to bear clearly in mind that "Self" here is not anything like what is generally understood by the English words "mind," "mental states," or even "soul" and individual "spirit." The "Self," as an equivalent of the ultimate Atman in man, is other than all mental states, other than even "spiritual" states, such as feelings of love, joy, charity, and the like, insofar as these also come and go, grow and decay, and are subject to change. The Atman is what substantiates these mental and spiritual states, so that they are then felt and experienced as the individual ego or "I."

Small Yet Great

As the Atman or ultimate Self in the individual, this ever-abiding, timeless Being is "smaller than the small" (*anor aniyan*), that is, infinitely small, and has no measurable magnitude. Anything that has a magnitude which can be measured, no matter how small the magnitude—anything, in other words, which is not either infinitely small or infinitely great —is perishable, is not abiding. There is no example anywhere in the universe of a thing of measurable magnitude which is at the same time ever-abiding and absolutely stable. And because the ultimate Being is stable, this Being, as Atman or the ultimate Self in man, is magnitudeless, is smaller than the smallest. And because the Atman in the individual is smaller than the smallest, is like a point (*anu*), we feel the Atman to be nowhere, located at no definite spot, and yet, as it were, everywhere in the body. Atman, the ultimate Self of man, seems to be present wherever attention, i.e., a particular mental function or movement, is directed.

At the same time, and paradoxical though it may seem, Atman as the abiding Being, is "greater than the great" (*mahato mahiyan*), that is, infinitely great. This is the reason why we can experience the universe as something spreading itself out in boundless space, and have also the feeling that we reach out even beyond the universe, beyond every limit which may be imagined in space. The ultimate Being in us seems to outrun the uttermost reaches of our senses.[4] It would be impossible to have these experiences if Atman were only "in-finitely small," like, say, a mathematical point.

But it might be thought that, in order to have the experience of wide-reachingness in space, Atman need not be infinitely great: a limited greatness (like the extent of the universe, which must, after all, be limited) would equally serve the purpose. This cannot be. For whatever is of limited extent and has therefore a measurable magnitude is, as noted above, perishable and cannot be abiding. But Atman is abiding Being; Atman, therefore, besides being infinitely small, must also be infinitely great; or, as the Vedic texts have it, Atman is both "smaller than the small" and "greater than the great." That is to say, Atman is beyond all space, everywhere and nowhere.

Being, Awareness, and Joy

Furthermore the ultimate Being is not an unconscious, unintelligent Being; on the contrary, the ultimate Being is Awareness (*chit*) itself. Because the ultimate Being is awareness, and because this Being is the real and ultimate experiencing subject in an individual, the latter is *aware* of anything objective, whether through the senses or only mentally. Awareness is felt, in experience, to belong to what abides in us as the ultimate ground of our existence and not to anything else which, even though a purely mental fact, can yet be experienced as something other than the Self, the experiencing subject.

The Being as Atman is also feeling. Feeling is the very root and ground of our existence as conscious entities. And this feeling is joyousness (*ananda*); to live and to be is joy; suffering is only when we are not able to live and to be as we would. Suffering is not the essential nature of Being, but joy (ananda) is; it is joy that is the root of all love and peace and bliss.[5]

Thus Atman, the ultimate Self in man, is pure Being (*sat*), objectless Awareness (*chit*), and unclouded Joy (*ananda*).

One Common Ground

And Atman, the ultimate Being, is timeless and spaceless.

As such, the ultimate Being is only one Being (*ekam sat*), one Atman in all individuals. There cannot be many ultimate Beings, many Atmans. Plurality has meaning only when there is any division either in time or space, or in regard to attributes.

In regard to attributes, the ultimate Being of one individual entity cannot in any way be distinguished from the ultimate Being of a different individual. The ultimate ground in one case is just as pure Being, Awareness, and Joy as in the other. Distinctions and differences in the attributes of individual subjects are caused only by the objective contents of experience, by what comes to be placed, as it were, in front of the pure Being and Awareness and seems to color the feeling of pure Joy. There can therefore be no distinction in regard to attributes between the Atman in one individual and that in another.

Nor can there be any division in Atman in regard to time and space. There can be no meaning in the statement that there are, *in different places,* different Atmans, all absolutely alike in regard to attributes and all infinitely great, i.e., all equally occupying every conceivable space, or, which is the same thing, all equally beyond every space limitation. It is equally meaningless to say that, while Atmans are all ever-abiding, there existed in the past some Atmans that have ceased to exist now, or that, while there are now other equally ever-abiding Atmans, they too will cease to exist in the future. Thus there is but one ultimate Being that is the one common ground, one Atman, one undivided Self, in every separate individual and in the universe.

This is held *not* as a matter of mere inference, but as a positive fact of experience on the part of men called Yogis and Rishis, who, it is maintained further, have been produced in an unbroken chain of succession down to this day, and whose positive experience and vision can be acquired by anyone, duly qualified, anywhere in any country and at any time. It is recognized, moreover, that this is the experience also of all true seers in other parts of the world who have been vaguely called "mystics."

This ultimate All-aware, All-joy Being, the Atman, the ultimate Self, both of the individual and of the universe and everything in it, is in reality beyond all predicates and names, as beyond all strictly logical formulation in thought. As such the Atman is referred to, in early Vedic texts, in a manner which is indefinite, no doubt intentionally. Atman is spoken of merely as "That One" and as the "One Being." But when a name is given, THAT is called Purusha, the Person; and in later literature *Uttama-Purusha* or *Purushottama*, the Supreme, the Ultimate Person within humanity and the universe.

The Atman is also called *Brahman*, though, strictly speaking, this name should be confined, as will be seen later, to a particular aspect of *Purusha*, the Ultimate Person.

Two Seeming Realities

We thus get *apparently* two fundamental realities or principles:

(1) Purusha as the one ultimate, timeless and spaceless Being and Self of humanity and the universe; and

(2) The system of ever-changing movements which constitute the universe and whatever is ever experienced as an object—movements which are apparently other than, and antithetical to, Purusha, the unchanging Being.

In reality, however, the system of movements, as the root of objectivity, is not a separate independent reality at all, but only Purusha appearing in a second role, but without ceasing, even for a moment, to be the abiding, unchanging, and unmoving Being that he in himself is. Movement without something moving has really no meaning. And what really moves, or rather appears to be moving, is only Purusha in another aspect—the aspect in which the endlessly enduring and the infinitely great, the timeless and spaceless Being appears, in the first instance, as the starting point of all that exists in time and space as well as of both time and space themselves. That is to say, Purusha appears as the infinitely small, or, to use a later expression, as the

"Benign Point" (*shiva bindu*). In other words, there is only one reality, only one principle, and that is Purusha; so that the root of objectivity is only Purusha in another phase, the phase of self-limitation, or, as it is called in the Vedas, the phase of "sacrifice" (*yajna*) — Purusha sacrificing ceaselessly by the ceaseless "negation" and the limitless "contraction" of his own timeless and spaceless Being, yet without suffering the least diminution or change in that ultimate Being that is himself.[6]

To put this in the language of the famous Purusha-Sukta section of the Rig-Veda, the aspect in which Purusha appears as the self-sacrificing source of the objective universe is, as it were, only a "quarter" of himself, while "three quarters" remain unmanifest beyond all objective thought and experience. That is to say, what appears as the universe is but a very limited aspect of Purusha, while what remains unmanifest is unlimited, is incomparably great. That this is the real significance of the Rig-Vedic text—which might be misconceived as meaning that Purusha is capable of an actual division, so that one measurable part appears as the universe while three equally measurable parts lie beyond—will be seen from another verse of the Vedas, perhaps a later one, which endeavors to define this relation between the two aspects of

Purusha in quite a different manner. In the form of a paradox, it declares:

That which lies beyond is Plenum, [full and undiminished]. That which appears as this here [i.e., as the universal] is also Plenum, equally full and un-diminished. Out from Plenum, Plenum arises. Plenum having been taken away out of Plenum, what remains is still the same [undiminished] Plenum. (Brih. Up. 5.1.)

The purport of this paradoxical statement is that Purusha, the timeless, spaceless Being, cannot possibly be really divided: the division, as unmanifest and manifest, is only apparent; Purusha in the aspect that becomes the universe is as full and complete as the aspect that transcends the universe and re-mains as ever undimmed and unchanged, with-out undergoing in any way any diminution whatsoever.

This is a state of affairs which cannot possibly be formulated in any logical statement what-soever without contradiction. Hence it is often spoken of as "indefinable" (*anirvacya*). It can, however, be made intelligible, at least partially if not fully, by an example or two.

One such example may perhaps be found in the domain of biology, in the division of a single vital cell into many. Here each new cell appears to have the same amount of material as the original one, apparently without any diminution, even when the original cell is divided many times over.

Another illustration of the process may perhaps be furnished by what is called in psychology "dissociation of personality." In this case, each new personality seems to be as complete and self-consistent as the one from which it is produced, and which, at the same time, seems to remain in every way unaffected.

A third illustration will perhaps be found in the sphere of physics. According to this, ions and electrons would seem to be but "points of strain" or "energy units" in a storehouse of universal energy, whether this storehouse be regarded as the "ether" formerly postulated by physics or as something else. As a center and fountain of energy, each of these "energy units" would seem to be as inexhaustible as the entire storehouse from which it is produced.

But perhaps the best example of the relation between the ultimate Being and its manifestation is to be found in the relation between what is recognized by psychologists in the West, practically universally, as the unconscious and the surface consciousness of a particular individual. The unconscious does not cease to exist as such when the surface consciousness has appeared. The surface consciousness behaves as though it were an entity quite apart from and independent of the unconscious, which, as a matter of fact, is its true being and ground. The two exist together, as it were, simultaneously, and while the surface consciousness has but little, if any, notion of its ground, the unconscious is fully aware of the former, which is, as it were, a child of the unconscious. The unconscious holds all that is "lost" and forgotten of the previous experiences as life of the individual, so that the "lost" memory of such experiences can be brought up to the surface consciousness by hypnotism and by yoga (to be explained later).

These are, however, only rough examples; and even if they represented quite a correct state of things in nature, they nevertheless could not be regarded as, in every respect, complete illustrations of the relation which subsists between the manifest and the unmanifest aspects of Purusha. In reality, this relation is one which, as said before, cannot be defined or described in any terms which will not be self-contradictory. Recognizing this limitation clearly, it may be said that it is one and the same Purusha, who in one aspect becomes the universe, while he yet remains entirely unchanged and undiminished in his true Being, which is the other aspect, away from and transcending the universe.

In the aspect as manifesting the universe, Purusha is given various names, of which the most usual is *Brahman,* sometimes translated as "the Word," which literally means "Word THAT which grows great,"[7] so that the unmanifest aspect has in later times been called *Parabrahman,* which should really mean what transcends Brahman.

To the manifesting aspect of Purusha are also given the names *Ish, Isha,* and *Ishvara,* all meaning "Lord."[8]

Thus it is this Brahman, "Word," or Isha, "Lord," who is really the Self, root, and origin of both the individual and the universe. That One, indeed, is the core of all that is: Ananda— Joy and Bliss and Love and Peace in one.[9] Hence do the Vedas proclaim:

> From Ananda, in truth, all Beings spring forth into existence; by Ananda, when born, they live; and unto Ananda they flee and enter. And again:
>
> Who, indeed, would move, who would breathe, if there were not this Ananda buried in the inmost space of every heart. For He alone, standing there, makes all life joyous and happy and blissful and loving.

Two Phases: Manifest and Potential

In other words, the universe, with everything in it, is only an outward flow and a crystallized form of the unceasingly upwelling Joy of Brahman.

But the present universe is not the only such manifestation. At some time in the past, no matter how remote, this universe came into existence, as surely as it shall end some day in the future, no matter how distant. Brahman, on the other hand, is timeless, an aspect of the timeless Purusha. Brahman has existed at all times, or, which is the same thing, beyond all times. It cannot, therefore, be that while Brahman had existed for all eternity without ever before manifesting a universe, That One suddenly appeared as this universe at some point of time, which, however long past, was but yesterday as compared with the timeless existence of Brahman. It is quite irrational to imagine that, having remained, as it were, idle all those countless aeons, timeless times, Brahman suddenly became this universe. The truth, on the contrary, is that Brahman has gone on appearing as universes forever without a beginning, so that the present universe is but one in a beginningless series, in which each succeeding universe is, as it were, a reincarnation of a

27

previous one that has perished.

Thus it happens that, as the Self of the universe, Brahman, like Purusha, has also a twofold phase:

(1) The phase of manifestation as the actual universe (this being called *shrishti,* "throwing out"; also *kalpa,* "imagining, or carving out");[10] and

(2) The phase in which the universe exists only in a potential form, just as the future tree exists in the seed (this being called *pralaya,* "absorption" or "dissolution").

It is between these two phases that Brahman, as the Self of the universe, has gone on alternating eternally, from beginningless time. The phase as an actual universe is a state of heterogeneous and multifarious objectivity, while the potential phase is a state of universal homogeneity, which is compared to an ocean, mighty and ever-flowing, but without a wave or ripple.[11]

The potential phase is also likened to a state of profound sleep, when Brahman, after universe-working exertion, is, as it were, at rest. To use the Vedic language, describing one such sleep and rest, previous to the emergence of this present universe: "By His own nature did That One breathe, though not a breath of wind was blowing."[12]

And if Pralaya, the potential state of the

universe, represents sleep on the part of Brahman, the fresh manifestation of a new universe is the waking-up anew of That One, or, which is the same thing, the waking-up of Atman as the Self of the Universe. Indeed, the successive stages (at least the first stages) through which Atman passes, till the uttermost physical objectivity is reached, are not unlike the stages of the swift mental journey of an individual person immediately on waking. This will be seen later when we come to consider how these stages come into existence. Let us, for the present, understand what they are. This can be done without much difficulty, because the stages, like the ultimate Being, are all present with us and always cooperating ceaselessly in every experience, however trivial, that we have in life.

Beginning at the physical—which is, as it were, the farthest removed from Atman in itself, and therefore the most veiled—and without noticing intermediate steps in the process, the "stages" may broadly be counted as follows:

A. The Manifest and the Unmanifest

Two factors which are different from each other as facts of experience, though not in essence, in much the same way as solids and liquids are different in experience, even though they may be *essentially* the same thing. These are:

(1) The Physical, which enters into the composition of our bodies, and also constitutes the material and basis of what we perceive through the bodily senses; these are known as the *bhutas,* or, as built up into the body of a living entity, *anna,* food.

(2) The Vital, which holds together the Physical in living things as an organic whole and makes it behave like a living entity, as distinguished from the "dead," or from what is called the "inorganic"; this is named *prana,* lit. "forthgoing," i.e., "responsive energy," "life."[13]

Of these again, the Physical is of two classes:

(a) A class of discrete entities, something like what physics calls "ions" and "electrons"; these are known as *paramanus* (the extremely, even infinitely, small things).

(b) A Continuum (or what looks like it), not unlike the "ether" which is, or at any rate formerly was, postulated by physicists as a sort of universal medium and background of all physical phenomena. It is called *akasha.*[14]

Paramanus

The Paramanus would be practically identical

with the ions and electrons of physics, if the latter were entities without a magnitude. Paramanus have "no inside and outside," and, when piled up so as to touch one another, produce only Paramanus. From this, it is clear that Paramanus are magnitudeless entities, practically like mathematical points; the ions and electrons of physics, on the other hand, have probably some magnitude—some length, breadth, and thickness—no matter how minute. It may not be impossible that modern physics may yet discover that ions and electrons, in case they have any magnitude, are only things derived, like atoms, from still simpler entities; and these latter, if magnitudeless, would then be the Paramanus as conceived from the Vedic point of view.

The other physical entity, the Continuum or Akasha, differs from the "ether" in that Akasha consists really of an infinite number of very rigid lines, called *dishah* (or, in the singular, *dish*), i.e., directions or pointers, which are figured in a different school of tradition as the "hair of Shiva."[15]

Of these again, it is the discrete Paramanus which, as stimuli moving and waving in various ways, are related especially to the four specific sensations of Temperature (heat and cold), Color, Flavor, and Odor. The Paramanus are therefore classed under four heads:

the Temperature-Stimuli
the Color-Stimuli
the Flavor-Stimuli
the Odor-Stimuli

They, again, in various groupings of more or less close cohesion, are related especially to the experiences of hardness, softness, weight, solidity, liquidity, and the like. From this point of view they are respectively named symbolically, or at any rate technically, Air, Fire, Water, and Earth, which are the so-called four "elements" of the philosophy of India and Greece. These names, in the technical sense and insofar at least as the philosophy of India is concerned, do not signify—and this cannot be too strongly emphasized—air, fire, water, and earth *as ordinarily understood*, but just the four classes of stimuli giving rise to the four specific sensations mentioned above.[16]

The Continuum

While the discrete Paramanus are thus ultimately responsible for the four specific sensations named above, or, as already suggested, they are the inferred, i.e., the "imagined," origin of the four types of sensation-forms, it is the Continuum or Akasha which is similarly responsible for the sensation of sound as we perceive it ordinarily.[17] Sound is not the essential and inalienable property of any discrete object anywhere that we know and experience in the universe: every one of the discrete objects can be absolutely silent, but none can absolutely affect others either as to temperature, or color, or flavor, or odor, or as to some combination of them. In other words, it is impossible to know any discrete objects whatsoever, except through one or the other of these sensation-forms; on the other hand, they can all be known without sound. And that is because sound is not the essential property of any of these. Sound is related specially to Akasha, is ethereal. This need not seem absurd now, in view of the daily broadcasting of messages and music by means of what is certainly not any of the discrete forms of matter.

As the ethereal Akasha fills all space, so that there is really no empty space in the absolute sense, the apparently empty spaces inside our bodies are full of Akasha, while the ponderable material therein is supplied by the four discrete groups of the Physical.

As regards the Vital (*prana*), its nature and functions will be considered later.

The only point to be noted here, in regard to the Physical (the material) and the Vital, is that we have them both in us.

Similarly in regard to the other stages in

the process of Atman becoming involved in objectivity; they are also in and with us always, in every experience of daily life, and may be enumerated as follows:

B. The Other Stages

(1) The Sense-powers (*Indriyas*) in two groups:
  (a) Those functioning through the nervous system; they may be called the Cognitive Senses (in Sanskrit, *jnanendriya*);
  (b) Those functioning through the muscles; they may be called the Reactive Senses or the Muscular Senses (in Sanskrit, *karmendriya*).

(2) Concrete Mentality (*Manas*)

(3) Sense-objects-in-general (*Arthas, Bhuta-matras,* or *Tan-matras*)

(4) The Ego-complex (*Vijñana, Buddhi,* or *Ahamkara*)

(5) The Universal Ideation (*Mahat* or *Mahat Atman*)

(6) Nothingness (*Asat, Avyakta,* or *Avidya*)

The Cognitive Senses

The Cognitive Senses (1) are the five obvious powers, or capacities, of hearing, feeling temperature (heat and cold), seeing, tasting, and smelling; while the Reactive Senses are the capacities of voicing, handling (touching and pressing), and locomotion, and of the voluntary muscular movements of rejecting from the body various forms of matter, especially liquids and solids.[18]

The only point about them that we need to note here is that, in the Vedic view, those powers are not identical with the physical bodily organs which are generally employed for their functioning; and that the powers are really independent of the physical organs, and belong to what is, as will be seen later, something other than the physical, i.e., to the limited "ego"; so that, when the particular physical organ by which one of these powers operates is damaged or destroyed, the latter can often still function in some other way. For instance, when the hand of a man is injured, he can yet handle things, say, by his feet.[19]

Concrete Mentality (*manas* in Sanskrit) (2) is that which shows itself, in one of its functions, as attention, without the cooperation of which the senses cannot function. As attention it is also selective, in that it selects, out of the multifarious sensation-stimuli impinging ceaselessly upon us from every direction, a few, which are "attended to," while the others are excluded (*vyavacchidya mano lakshayati*), so that none but the selected group is transformed into a particular sensation or group of sensations. When, for instance, a person is watching a performance in a circus tent, let us say, in the middle of a busy town, and does not notice the noise of traffic outside, it is not that the sound-stimuli from the streets are not pouring in upon him or her, but that those stimuli are not being transformed into sound-forms, because the person's Concrete Mentality (Manas) has excluded them at the time and has fixed itself as attention on that particular group of stimuli which are being transformed as the circus performance that is being observed.

Concrete Mentality, moreover, is also that which, in addition to selecting a particular group or groups of sense-stimuli, builds up "concrete" sense-forms or images—visual, auditory or otherwise—out of the stimuli so selected.[20] It is this Concrete Mentality (Manas) in the absence of which we are absent-minded, so that we fail to notice an object even when it is, as it is said, right before us. Thus the presence in us of this Concrete Mentality (Manas) is quite obvious in every act of sense perception.

The presence in us, or in relation to us, of

the next group, the Sense-objects-in-general
(3), is somewhat difficult to detect. They may,
however, be inferred, as the standards to
which constant references are made whenever
we experience a sensation such as a sound
or a color or any other. We experience these
only as particulars—as one variety among
others, all belonging to a general class. Thus,
in the matter of color, what we actually perceive are the varieties red, blue, yellow, and
the like, which are all so different from one
another. Yet we regard them all, as it were,
instinctively, as of the same class, color-in-
general. Of color-in-general, however, we have
no direct experience anywhere in our ordinary
life; nor can we picture vividly to ourselves
this color-in-general or any other sensation-
in-general. Yet there must be somewhere, in
or in relation to some part of our individual
being, this color-in-general and every other
sensation-in-general; otherwise they could
never be thought of. The exact nature of this
relation will be considered later. All we need
to note here is that the sensation-generals do
exist somewhere. The Yogis maintain that
they are directly and positively experienced
when a certain stage in the unfoldment of
the superconscious is reached by means of the
true yoga discipline.[21]

The Ego-Complex

The next item, the Ego-complex (4) or simply the ego, the limited "I," is that factor in us as individuals which, as one of its functions, supplies all that is needed to substantiate a sensation-form—as what is actually "given" by a sense or senses—so as to make of it a particular object. Thus, for instance, when we say we see a red rose from a distance, what is actually given at the moment by the sense of sight is nothing but a stream of red color points, made into the form of a rose by the operation of the Concrete Mentality (Manas). And it is, therefore, not yet what we really mean by a red rose, which is not only the red color we actually see but also several other attributes associated with, and, as it were, placed under, the color-form as its supporting frame, its substance. These are, for instance, the attributes of softness, coolness, light weight, fragrance (which, let us suppose, we are not actually smelling at the time, being far away from the rose), and the like. A rose means all these and much more and not merely the patch of color we actually see. And as we associate these attributes with what is actually given by the sense of sight at the time, they are really brought out from some part of our being; and we can so bring them out only because they are stored there as facts of actual experiences of all these attributes of the rose, experiences gained not merely by seeing roses from a distance, but by handling and smelling them. The part of our nature where these and similar other facts of concrete experiences are held together—arrogated, retained as one's own—is the ego, which is nothing but a "bundle" of the actual experiences of things concrete kept cohering together by the feeling of "my and mine."

Its Vedic name, *vijñana*, i.e., various bits of experiences (*jñana*) held together as an organic whole and unit, is thus quite appropriate. In the Sankhya and most other post-Vedic writings it is called *Ahamkara*, the "Ego-Creature,"[22] the ego as something created and built up.

Universal Ideation

The presence of the next item (5) is revealed in the positive and emphatic judgment (*buddhi*): "This is a rose, not anything else." Such a judgment is possible not only because we are able to refer the particular rose now before us—having been built in the way mentioned above—to the ideal rose, and to the ideal flower, i.e., to rose as a class and to flower as a class, but also to the class not-rose, i.e., to everything else in the universe other than the ideal rose. This means there is something in us which is universal and, however unconscious, is always present. This something provides as the standard of reference not only the ideal rose and the ideal flower but also the ideal everything. It is to this ideal standard that an instant reference is made when the present rose is recognized as belonging to the class "rose" and to the class "flower" and, finally, as outside the whole of the remaining universe.

This universal standard of reference, which is really a great and universal ideation of everything possible, enabling us to form a positive judgment, is called *Mahat*, "the Mighty," or *Mahat Atman*, "the Mighty Self," of our individual lives.

Nothingness

The final factor, or stage (final when counted up from the Physical but first from the standpoint of a new universal manifestation) is the Power of Negation (6). It shows itself as ever present with us not only when we form a positive judgment of the type mentioned above, but as the power which sends us to sleep every day of our lives and ceaselessly obliterates things and objects from our view, so that none can remain forever before our gaze as limited entities, even though our inmost Self, our ultimate Being, is Awareness itself, boundless, timeless, and spaceless. On the other hand, if it were not for this Power of Negation ceaselessly operating in us there would be no endeavor and no movement in life, which from the Vedic point of view is but a ceaseless seeking of that Joy (Ananda) of which we have somewhere had a foretaste, but which is now lost, taken away, suppressed, and wrought into Nothing by this Power of Negation.

It shows itself in a positive and emphatic judgment, such as "this is a rose and nothing else," insofar as this judgment involves the negation, suppression, and putting away from experience of everything else but the rose, the "everything" here being constituted by the Universal Ideation considered above.

The Factors of Human Existence

These then are the stages—counted in the reverse order—of Atman's march away from the true state of That One until Atman's appearance as the Physical is reached. And the stages are all contained in every one of us, constituting the various factors of our individual existence. Thus:

The Physical constitutes the physical body.

The Vital (Life), the Sense Powers and Sensation-generals, the Concrete Mentality (Manas) and the Ego constituting what is generally called the individual soul—that which differentiates one individual from another in character, mentality, and the like (Subtle Typical Body, the *sukshmadeha* or *lingadeha* of the Darshanas).

The Universal Ideation as synthesizing and unifying, i.e., bridging all gulfs of separation, is what is later termed the Causal Body (*karanadeha*), that which makes us love and feel ourselves as one with all; it may perhaps be said to correspond to what St. Paul calls *spirit* in his threefold division into body, soul, and spirit.

The Principle of Negation or Sacrifice, or rather self-sacrifice, is, as will be seen later, the same as *Shabda-Brahman*, the Universal sound-Word, and its presence in us will be explained later. It may be said to correspond to the Logos or the Christ principle of Christian teaching.

Finally the Abiding Being stands as the background of all experience as the one ultimate Self in us all.

Counted in the order of their coming out into existence, these stages or principles, constituting the body, soul, spirit, and the divine in us, may be stated as follows:

(1) Nothingness (*Asat, Avyakta, Avidya, Aja, Maya* in the Vedas; *Prakriti, Pradhana,* and *Shakti* in the Sankhya and the Tantras).

(2) Universal Ideation, or simply Ideation, or the Ideal (*Mahat, Mahat Atman*).

(3) Ego-Creature or ego, i.e., the bundle of concrete experiences held together as an organic unit, and behaving as such, felt as the local and temporal "I"—as "I am now here," "I am John Smith" (*Vijñana, Ahamkara*).

  (a) Concrete Mentality (*Manas*)
  (b) Sensation-Generals (*Bhuta-matras; Tan-matras*)
  (c) Sense-Powers (*Indriyas*)
  (d) The Vital (*Prana*)

(4) The Physical Bhutas, the "Have-becomes," as the last things in the process of becoming limited.[23]

And they come about in something like the following manner.[24]

Waking Up

Waking up, as it were, from a long slumber in the state of universal homogeneity (*pralaya*), Atman "glances round" (*ikshati*), so to say, and finds nothing existing,[25] quite forgetful of the fact that Atman itself is. It may be com-

43

pared to the experience of one who, let us say, went to sleep at a place which was then full of things, but now is completely empty of them, and who wakes up to this emptiness. The first thought on waking is *not* oneself, but the emptiness around one. In much the same way, Atman beholds *not* THAT but Nothingness, to which Atman glances round. This glancing round on the part of Atman now, and experiencing Nothingness, is the "Primary Deliberation" (*para vimarsha*); it is the first fluttering, waving, vibrating Thought (*prathama spanda*); and, as a vibrating, waving Thought-Energy, it is also the Primary Word (*brahman*), the Primary Sound (*shabda*), and Name (*nama*). Forgetful as Atman is of itself at this stage, this is an act of self-negation (*nishedha-vyapara*) and self-sacrifice (*yajna*) —an act of great strength and might (*shakti*). It is this, therefore, which most probably constitutes what is called in Christianity the Logos, or the Christ principle, which is really a principle of self-sacrifice and love.

But this very experience of Nothingness leads to the next stage, which is that of calling up before the ever-aware gaze of Atman all that was in the past, i.e., the universe as it existed before. This now rises up as a "Mighty Vision."[26]

It is likened, in the Sankhya writings, to the thought-experience of objectivity on waking up from sound sleep (*suptotthita-cittavat*) on the part of an individual, such as mentioned earlier, who went to sleep in the midst of a scene of beautiful objects of infinite variety but on waking finds it quite empty. As he or she glances round and beholds emptiness, he or she naturally remembers all that there was before. It is in a manner somewhat like this that the experience of the previous universe rises up as a Mighty Vision at the stage we are now considering. At the same time it is a vision of what is to be, and therefore the pattern, complete and perfect, of the universe that is to appear presently in space and time. Hence it is the Ideal and the Archetypal, a Vision of Beauty (*rupa*, which also means color and form).

While this survey of the ideal universe is going on—Atman being thus far quite self-forgetful, lost in the contemplation of the Universal Vision—the latter fades away, disappears from view by the operation of the negating energy which, as we have seen, is always present. This disappearance of the Vision leads Atman to turn inward as the Experiencer of the Vision, even though it is no longer there. Thus a distinction between the Self as the Experiencer, the subject, and the Vision as the experienced object, arises for the first time; and by this very distinction, thus realized, Atman becomes limited, regarding the Self as something *other* than the Vision—becomes, as it were, one of two things, which means limitation and no longer the unlimited all-in-all. In other words, Atman now becomes the limited I, the individual ego. This experience is also one of *movement* away from the Vision and then again toward it in search of it; that is to say it is Karma (activity, movement to and fro).

With these three—Name and Form (Word and Beauty, *nama* and *rupa*) previously mentioned, together with Karma—we get all the fundamentals of our experience of the objective universe.

Before proceeding further, however, with our brief description of the Process, which in the systematized Vedanta is called *vivarta*, "rolling out," it may be well to note here an important point in connection with the appearance and disappearance of the various phases of experience. It is this: that "disappearance" here does not mean absolute destruction or absolute nonexistence. On the contrary, in regard to these stages, the same principle holds good as in the relation between the unmanifest (transcendent) and the manifest (immanent) Purusha. We have noted above how, in the Vedic view, the unmanifest does not cease to be, even when the manifest comes out into existence. They both are, as it were, simultaneously. Following the same principle, even when Nothingness (*asat, avyakta*) comes into existence, Atman exists also, though, as it were, on a different plane, and, so to say, unnoticed by Nothingness. Nothingness, or, which is the same thing, the Awareness of the Nonexistence of anything, is as much an entity as—indeed, more so than—an individual person is, both being, so to speak, equally ensouled by Atman. As a matter of fact, all the stages are, as it were, so many entities, all conscious and feeling, though in varying degrees. As conscious entities, they are given appropriate names, such as Hiranyagarbha, Prajapati, Prajñatman, Prajñanatman, Prajña, Sutratman, Shakti, and the like.[27]

The Stages as Simultaneous

And all these stages or entities exist, as it were, simultaneously, but in different planes, because conditions of time and space are not the same everywhere, as will be seen later. Simultaneity, therefore, cannot have the same meaning in regard to the relation of one stage to another as it has with respect to the mutual relations of facts and factors in one and the same stage. The stages exist, rather, in different space-time frames, to borrow an expression from the language of Relativity. Moreover, while there can be no subsequent stage in existence unless all the anterior stages exist, informing and en-souling the subsequent stage, as it were, yet every anterior stage can exist without what comes after it. Thus there can be no physical stage without all the antecedent ones existing as its ground or soul. The stage of Nothing-ness, on the contrary, can exist without there being any of the subsequent appearances. In the same way, Brahman or Purusha can and does always exist in a true state, even without Nothingness or the universe. But the universe, from Nothingness onward, can never be with-out Purusha as the uttermost ground.

Thus it happens that when, by the operation of the Power of Negation (existing and working, as it were, from within), the Universal Vision vanishes from the view of Atman and Atman becomes the limited ego, the Vision, like Nothingness and Purusha, does not cease to exist, but continues in its own plane.

Powers of Cognition

The ego, the limited I, therefore, begins again to seek out[28] this lost, but unconsciously existing, Vision. The Vision can, however, no longer appear as a whole, as in the previous stage when the experiencing subject is one and undivided with the Vision in every part and aspect. It can now be remembered and pictured only in parts and bits and in different facets, inasmuch as the ego can see it only as an outside observer, and, as it were, from particular angles and therefore never as a whole Vision, never in all its dimensions.

And these bits and facets of the universal Vision, as they appear before the seeking ego, become the "sensations-in-general" or "sensation-generals" (*Bhuta-matra*) out of which, as will be seen presently, the fully diversified and completely objectified universe is built up.

These sensation-generals are only five, as stated above, namely:

Sound-in-general (i.e., Sound undifferentiated)

Temperature-in-general

Color-in-general

Flavor-in-general

Odor-in-general

They are all produced from the ego, drawn out, as though from its unconscious depths, as facets of the lost Universal Vision.

These sensation-generals are, as said above, the standards to which, in everyday life, an instant reference is made, as soon as one senses a particular variety of sound, temperature, color, flavor, or odor. They are, as we may say, the general concepts of these diversified and particularized sensations and cannot ordinarily be pictured to our mind, any more than there can be pictured, let us say, triangularity or humanity or kindness. We call up only *particular* concrete images—particular triangles, particular human beings, particular acts of kindness, and the like—when we imagine we are picturing these things in themselves in their general abstract forms. In reality, we are in touch with the sensation-generals in a deeper part of our nature as individuals than in the purely physical world. And they come into existence, in the way described above, prior to the physical.

But as they come into existence, they also draw out from the ego the corresponding capacities or powers with which they are apprehended, i.e., they draw out the senses, or rather sense-powers. Indeed, the sensation-generals may be said to be but one end of a single composite phenomenon of which the sense-powers (*indriya*) represent the other side.

Corresponding to the sensation-generals, therefore, the sense-powers are, as mentioned before, also five:

the power of hearing
the power of sensing temperature
the power of seeing

the power of tasting

the power of smelling

We may call them, as suggested above, by the general name of "cognitive senses" or "cognitive powers" (as a translation of the Sanskrit term *jñanendriya*).

Powers of Action

With the appearance of these, there are also brought into existence, out from the ego, the powers of reacting to what is apprehended by means of the cognitive senses.

These powers of reacting or powers of action (designated in Sanskrit by the term *karmendriya*) are similarly five, as said before, namely: the power of voicing (as the reaction to hearing sound); the power of touching, i.e., putting one's hand, as it were, on the spot where the sensation of heat or cold or a tickling sensation is felt (reaction to temperature sensation); the power of locomotion, i.e., running away from or toward what appears suddenly as an objective vision (reaction to seeing color); and the two muscular efforts to eject from the physical body liquid, solid, and other forms of physical materiality. Reactive powers express themselves, in all instances, as muscular efforts, including the effort of "pressing," giving rise to the experience of hardness, softness, and the like, as said before. The reactive powers thus correspond, in certain of their aspects, to what is known as the muscular sense in psychology as it is studied in the Occident.

Concrete Mentality

Along with these various sense-powers, both cognitive and reactive, there appears also from the ego another power which is the most general of them all and without which not one of them can function, namely Manas, or the Concrete Mind, considered above. As already pointed out, it shows itself constantly as the power which, cooperating with one or other of the sense-powers, selects at a given moment only certain of the streams of impacts pouring in upon us from all directions of the objective world. Excluding others, it makes of the selected impacts the various sensation-forms of which we are directly aware, i.e., which constitute the actually "given" of the senses, in regard to any particular form of perception. It is really a movement, a waving to and fro, of the seeking here and there (*eshana*, desire), which is the Manas, Concrete Mentality, when the movement assumes the form of an entity (a particle, as the Vaisheshika views it). It is much the same as the way the ultimate constituents of physical matter are now regarded by science as both waves and particles.

Vitality

The next item to be considered is Vitality, or Prana. It is what differentiates, in experience, the living from the nonliving. We may therefore call it simply Life.

This Life has, in the Vedic view, a fivefold function:

Appropriation (*prana*)[29]
Rejection or Elimination (*apana*)
Assimilation (*samana*)
Distribution (*vyana*)
Regeneration (*udana*)

The four first-named functions are obvious. As long as there is Life in the body these are continually going on. To begin with, Life is a selective process. It appropriates, takes into the system, a certain quantity of material which it needs for building up and maintaining the organism in which it operates. It also rejects from the system what is not useful. One of the manifestations of this double activity of Life is seen in the ceaseless processes of breathing in and breathing out, which have therefore been taken as the most characteristic feature of living creatures and even regarded as the equivalent of Life (Prana). What is selected is further *assimilated* to that form (as for instance, blood) in which it can be built into the system. This activity is compared to that of fire, namely combustion, so that the result is said to rise up like a sevenfold flame. The fourth function is also apparent in that the assimilated material, such as blood, is distributed all over the body, by means of channels radiating from the heart[30] to every part of the body.

The fifth type of function will require a little explanation. In one form, it is what serves as a link between the Life in the individual and the Life universal, which, as explained below, is Brahman. It is therefore said, metaphorically, that in dreamless sleep, produced by the operation of the self-negating Maya, we are "taken up daily to Brahman,"[31] so that we thereby have our tired vitality refreshed, or, as one might say, regenerated. This is done by replenishing, as it were, our individual tanks of Life from Brahman, the universal ocean of Life, when, as in dreamless sleep, all diversified objectivity vanishes from our consciousness, and thus outlets of Life in us are for the time being largely shut off.

That function of Life which thus, as it were, carries us up to Brahman and enables us to have our stores of Life daily regenerated is the fifth function, called *udana*, the "upgoing."

Reincarnation

It also appears in another form, in the process of what is known as reincarnation of the soul (as defined above), in that it carries what is really the individual in us (apart from our physical bodies), as our soul is, from one sphere of existence into another, from one death to a new birth. In the Vedic view the individual in oneself, i.e., the individual soul, is, to repeat, only the group of ever-changing factors, from ego downward to Life, held together as a unit against the background of the one universal Being, the one ultimate Self in all. But though ever-changing, this group still maintains a certain self-identity and continuity, so that it can be felt and spoken of as the *same* entity in spite of the change, in much the same way as the physical body, although ceaselessly changing, can be still spoken of as one and the same body from birth to death. The only difference is that while the body is produced at birth (or conception) and perishes at death, the soul associated with a particular body comes into existence long before the body—the soul having been created by the process of manifestation in the way described—and continues to exist, even after the death of the body, as one and the same entity in the sense defined above.

This type of self-identity and continuity is maintained by the soul even when not connected with a physical body and, as it were, floating in space between a death and new birth, in much the same way as a piece of music, broadcast into space, maintains its self-identity and individuality even when rushing through the electro-magnetic field, so that it can be reproduced as the same music by means of a suitable receiver. The soul, in this sense and thus maintaining its self-identity, is born and dies again and again, until it reaches a stage in which that aspect of Purusha, the ultimate Being, standing behind the soul as its ground and, as it were, involved in it—having forgotten himself in the way described above—remembers his true identity and ceases any longer to identify in feeling with the soul. When this state is reached the soul perishes, just as a particular body does at death. This is the state of experience when the self-forgetful Being, recollecting itself in a positive experience, realizes and proclaims the truth "THAT am I," "I am the Divine."[32] Until this experience, called Release or Freedom (*moksha*), is gained, the "soul" is born again and again; and as this takes place, it is carried from one state of existence into another by means of Life functioning in the fifth way as Udana.[33]

In other words, death and rebirth of the soul are regarded as only different forms of the same phenomena of dreamless sleep and waking up which occur in the everyday life of the individual; and the movement to and fro in connection with both groups of phenomena is accomplished by the soul by means of Life functioning in its regenerative mode, which is Udana.

Life

This Life is therefore given a very important place in the Vedic view of things. Indeed, it is often identified with Atman and Brahman, while it is spoken of in one place as coming into existence from Atman directly without the intervention of any other stage and is regarded as having the same relation to Atman as the shadow has to the body. Besides, all things are said to be established in Life. Life is, in other words, the same as Brahman, the Universal Word or Sound, and the same movement as the latter.[34] But insofar as it operates in the individual, it comes into manifestation after the appearance of Manas, the Concrete Mentality, because it is Manas which as a seeking principle (*eshana*) is the seat of desire, attention, and interest, and because it is by an unconscious act of this desire, attention, and interest that Life functions in an individual and his or her body. For this reason we are told that Life comes into this body by the operation of the Manas.[35] For the same reason also we are further told that when we learn, by means of yoga, to remove even unconscious desire for and interest in the body, we can die at will, just as the body can be kept alive as long as we desire.[36]

The Physical

With the appearance of Life, as it operates in the individual, we have reached the stage in the process of manifestation where we find that all the elements of the superphysical universe, the realms of what is called the Spirit and the Soul, are ready. We have now to consider only the final step wherein the Physical is produced. We have seen that the Physical consists of the ethereal, all-pervading Akasha as the medium of Sound and four other groups of stimuli connected with the four sensations of Temperature-feeling (heat and cold), Color, Flavor, and Odor, symbolically called Air, Fire, Water, and Earth. These are collectively the five Bhutas and are produced from the five sensation-generals, called Bhutamatras (later Tanmatras), inasmuch as they have no other meaning except the inferred, i.e., the imagined origins or concomitants, moving or stationary, of the sensations of Sound, Temperature, Color, Flavor, and Odor as they are actually perceived by means of the senses operating in the physical body, i.e., as varieties of these sensations as distinguished from the general ones. And they are produced in the following manner:[37]

Prior to the appearance of the Physical, the objects of experience perceived by means of the senses—which have already come into existence in the way described above—are, as we have seen, of a general character, such as sound-in-general, temperature-feeling-in-general, color-in-general, and the like. There are as yet no variations in them. Owing, however, to the operation of the Principle of Negation (Asat, Avidya) which is always present with the soul, they gradually cease to be noticed and then disappear altogether from experience, in much the same way as Universal Ideation (Mahat) disappeared from experience at an earlier stage when the limited I was produced.

Just as then the Self, as it were, groped about in search of the vanished Universal, but found in its place only broken facets and fragments in the shape of the sensation-generals, so the Soul, seeking in a similar manner to refind the lost generals, discovers only bits and facets of them. This is because the Self as soul has now to work under a still further limitation, namely, that of Manas, the Concrete Mentality, which at this stage covers it up as in a cloak,[38] and makes it labor, as will be seen presently, under different conditions of space and time, in a different space-time frame. In other words, the sensation-generals, now being experienced through the medium of Manas, appear before the soul in their different variations, much as the white sunlight appears in the many colors of the spectrum when seen through a prism. Thus sound-in-general appears as varieties of sound, temperature-feeling-in-general as degrees of temperature, and the like.

And it is with the experience of these variations in the five general sensations that there also appear, as consequences, the five Bhutas that we are now considering. For a proper understanding of these stupendous consequences, let us place ourselves, in imagination, in a position similar to that in which the newly produced soul finds itself before it receives its first physical embodiment. We shall begin with the origin of Akasha, Ethereal Space.

Part I

Characteristics of the Soul

At the start let us make clear one very important point regarding certain fundamental characteristics of the Soul which, or rather who, is now a full-fledged Individual constituted of the previously produced ego and Manas (Concrete Mentality), all the powers of sensation and action (*indriya*), and vitality (*prana*).

Buried within the Soul, as it were, are not only Atman, but also the previous stages of Nothingness (Asat, Avidya) and Vision (Mahat), while the Ego is its central point, its nucleus and core. And they all show themselves as three well-defined tendencies or characteristics of the soul.

Of these, the ego (Ahamkara) is really a principle of movement, having come into existence as the result of Atman moving away, as it were, from the Vision (Mahat) to itself, as the subject of and distinguished from the Vision. And it shows itself constantly as such, i.e., as the tendency to run and jump about like a monkey.[39] This is called, in the technical language of systematized philosophy, *Rajas* (flaring up like red fire or dust).

Vision is the principle of *looking round*, it having come into existence by Atman looking round, as it were, after the experience of

61

Nothingness. This is later technically called *Sattva* (Existence).

Nothingness is the principle of negation, restriction, and contraction by which Purusha limits, restricts, contracts, and negates himself, as it were, so as to have the experience "Nothing is" (*na vidyate kim api*), forgetting even himself, forgetting that he is. This is later technically called *Tamas* (Darkness).[40]

Sound and Ethereal Space

After this necessary digression, let us now consider the origin of Akasha, Ethereal Space. Let us imagine ourselves to be present face to face with, or rather to be immersed in, a sea of homogeneous sound which has already become, for the reason stated above, no sound at all, that it, has ceased to form an object of perception. Let us also imagine that there are no other objects whatsoever, as would be the case under the circumstances we are trying to picture—the other sensation-generals having equally and for the same reasons ceased to be perceived. Then let us further imagine that there suddenly arises, or, which is the same thing, is suddenly perceived, a variety of sounds. What would be the experience that would instantly, instinctively, and necessarily follow this perception of a variety of sounds? They would be experienced all over the soul, there being as yet no physical body and no localized senses to perceive them.

The answer from the Vedic point of view is that the consequent experience will be that of something going in *all directions* and filling the universe, i.e., Ethereal Space. In other words, with the experience of varieties in sound there is produced Ethereal Space. This happens in the following manner:

Simultaneously with the perception of varieties of sound, the soul will, under the influence of Rajas and working through Manas, at once *run out* everywhere, imagining that the perceived sounds are coming from all directions, corresponding to the experience of the sound as being all over the soul. In other words there would be produced the notion of all directions imagined as straight, rigid lines going everywhere—imaginary lines no doubt, but very important ones.[41]

But, as we can learn from our daily experience, the mind and senses, even though sent out under the influence of Rajas, cannot run out forever. The pull from behind, of Tamas, is also always present in the Soul. The mind therefore turns back after reaching a certain point in its outward run and is compelled, owing to the centripetal pull of Tamas, to come back home to the center of the soul. As it does so, however, it follows a course that is curved and coiling, owing to the influence of Sattva. That this is how the mind works will be evident to any person endeavoring to concentrate the mind, i.e., to bring it to the central point of the Soul. The meditator will find that this cannot be done at once; the mind cannot be brought back, as it were, in a straight line. It hovers round for a time and then only comes to rest either in concentration, if the soul is strong, or in sleep.

It thus happens that the mind, after ceasing to chase the sounds to the farthest possible limits of its running capacity, comes back to the soul by paths that, as it were, coil round the straight lines already produced by the outgoing tendency of Rajas.

The result is a most complicated structure. First there are these countless rigid straight lines going out in all directions—away from the Soul as from a radiating center. For the Soul, i.e., the limited Atman, can move in all directions simultaneously even when related to a physical body; we can all verify this by listening to sounds all around us.

Second, these lines turn back after reaching a certain point on the outward run. These turning points thus constitute, for the Soul that is spinning the lines out, the outer surface of the sphere of experience which is his or her universe.

Third, each of the returning lines, as they return, coil round the straight ones.

Thus the lines, straight and curved, produce in their totality a most complex structure— rather a marvelous piece of webbing. This fabric thus woven is the Ethereal Space and serves as the frame, the locale, for all physical experiences of the particular Soul. All objects experienced by the Soul are held before that Soul in different positional relations by the lines (*dishah*) of the Ethereal Space.[42]

Though all imaginary, this Ethereal Space is for the Soul very real and rigid, and works, so long as it is not again transcended by yoga as explained below. And it is produced from the perception of variety in the sensation of sound-in-general in the way explained.[43]

This picture of the inner structure of Ethereal Space is symbolized in various ways which it is not possible to explain here. There is, however, one particular form of symbolism which may be noted. It is that of the sacred Kusha grass. Quantities of this straight, line-like grass, representing the lines of living energy as the constituent elements of Ethereal Space, are spread on sacred sands, which again symbolize Atman in the aspect of points con- stituting the lines. On the grass thus spread out there is lighted even now, in Brahmanical ceremonies, the sacrificial fire representing the universal Fire that burns on the altar of Ethereal Space—that Fire into whose secret Nachiketas was initiated by Yama, and which the seers and Yogins behold in their inmost being as Tejas, Light of boundless, spaceless, timeless Life and Awareness.[44]

It may not be impossible that the fire burning in the bush, visioned by Moses, may have been this universal spiritual Fire burning in the midst of the bush of these rigid lines of Akasha —of firmament—radiating from the center of Being, who is again conceived in some forms of symbology as a mountain (*parvata*).[45]

This appearance of Akasha in the way mentioned above is described technically in some of the systems of philosophy by the statement: "From the variations produced in the Bhuta-matra of Sound there comes into manifestation Ethereality, or Ether (Akasha)."

This is said because there need be no other experience whatsoever for the realization of the varieties of Sound but that of all directions, or, which is the same thing, of an indefinite something going out in all directions. There may be other experiences, as indeed there will be at a later stage; but these need not be there or necessarily precede that of Akasha.

Part I

Temperature (Air)

Next let us suppose that we are immersed in a sea of uniform temperature which has already ceased to be perceived as an object, and that there are as yet no other objects but the already produced varieties of Sound, as would be the case under the circumstances we are considering. Then let us further suppose that there arises a variety in this uniform and homogeneous temperature, and we begin to feel it to be more hot or more cold, a freezing or a burning sensation. What would be the necessary and inevitable experience accompanying or following this variation in the sensation of temperature? It would be, says the Vedic tradition, the experience of "ticklish" movements like a gentle aerial current. And it is this experience which is technically Air (Vayu). There need not necessarily be any other experience whatsoever for the realization of variations in temperature but that of this gentle air-like flow, although there may be—as later there will be—other experiences as well, accompanying that of variations in temperature. In other words, from the experience of variation in Temperature-in-general there arises the experience of Air, or, which is the same thing, there is produced Air.

67

Speaking technically, from the variations produced in the Bhuta-matra of Temperature there comes into manifestation Aeriality, or Air (*vayu*).

Color: Form and Shape (Fire)

Again let us suppose that we are face to face with an all-enveloping mass of Color-in-general, which, for reasons mentioned above, has already ceased to form an object of experience, although there may be present in the experience, at this stage, the already produced perceptions of the varieties of Sound and Temperature, and consequently, Ethereal Space and Air. Then let us imagine that there suddenly arises the experience of a variety of colors. What would be the necessarily consequent experience when this is realized? The obvious answer would perhaps be that it is the experience of Form and Shape (*rupa*). But a little reflection will show that it would really be the experience of a something, some power or energy, which builds up, transforms, or destroys forms. For when there suddenly arises a patch of color in the vacancy of the horizon, it is no doubt seen as a shape or form of some sort. But this form may be said to be the same thing as the color, because without it, color, as thus perceived at the time, has hardly any meaning. Therefore the perception of colors of this type means really the same thing as the perception of forms; so much so that, instead of saying that there arose the experience of a variety of colors, one might as well say that there arose the experience of a variety of forms.[46]

The experience of form, therefore, cannot be called a consequent experience in the same way as Ethereal Space (Akasha) is the consequent experience to that of a variation in Sound-in-general or the experience of Aeriality is consequent to that of variation in Temperature-in-general. The experience which is really a consequent one in this case is that of a something, some power, energy, or movement which produces, transforms, or destroys the forms.

This form-producing energy or movement is technically called Fire (Agni), by which term, however, we must not understand— and this cannot be too strongly emphasized, in view of the numerous and gross misconceptions that have been formed of its meaning —anything but this energy or power of which the only function is combustion or chemical action (*jvalana* or *paka*). Again this means simply building up, producing or reproducing, and destroying shapes, bringing shapes and forms into existence from what is formless, and changing one form into some other or others and vice versa.

It is thus from the experience of variety in Color-in-general that there arises the experience of Fire. Or, speaking technically, from the variations produced in the Bhuta-matra of Color there comes into manifestation Fire (*agni*), the Form-builder.

Flavor (Water)

Next let us imagine that our experience of Flavor-in-general, which has already ceased to be an object of perception, changes into that of a variety of flavors. The necessary experience consequent on this would be, as can easily be seen, that of movement, as of moisture, i.e., liquidity; for what is tasted, different flavors, is always found associated with the feeling of moisture, without any other sensation so necessarily accompanying it. It is this experience of moisture or liquidity thus produced which is technically and symbolically called Water (Ap). It is therefore stated: From the variations produced in the Bhuta-matra of Flavor there comes into manifestation Water (*ap*). This may appear strange, and even absurd, in view of the fact that, unlike the senses of sight, hearing, and temperature-feeling, the sense of taste plays such a small and unimportant part. It does not seem possible that, from this comparatively un-important experience of tasting a variety of flavors, there can be produced, so vast a result as the experience of liquidity, which forms so great a part of the physical world.

But we must not forget that, at the stage we are considering, there is as yet no physical body of the Soul, and the senses are therefore not localized in the body. Therefore the sense of taste and that of smell are, like all the other senses, all over the soul, as it were. Moreover the Self, in these stages, feels itself to be but a nonspatial point (*anu*), since the Self has now ceased to feel itself to be the infinitely great and cannot be anything of measurable dimensions, inasmuch as all measurable forms are perishable and the Self is not. These sensations of taste and smell are therefore at this stage as all-filling and overwhelming as any others.

There is thus nothing really absurd in the idea that Water, i.e., what is perceived as moist or liquid, is produced from the experience of variation in Flavor-in-general.

Odor (Earth)

Finally let us suppose that our experience of Odor-in-general is, similarly and under similar circumstances, changed into that of a variety of odors. The necessary experience consequent on this would be not that of "all directions," nor of Air or Fire, nor even of anything liquid or watery, although all these may be, and indeed often are, present at the time. None of these need, however, be present. The only experience which is absolutely necessary and is necessarily present is simply that of a something standing still, staying, or sticking, as it were, to the sense of smell, but felt at this stage all over the soul. It is, in other words, an experience of something stable, of stability, which is the essential characteristic of all things solid and hard, i.e., earthy, of the nature of Earth. We may therefore say that with the experience of variety in Odor-in-general there is also produced the experience of stability or solidity from which again come all such experiences as hardness, roughness, pressure or weight, and so on, i.e., all that is meant by the technical Earth (*prithivi*).[47]

Or, as it may be stated technically: From the variations produced in the Bhuta-matra of Odor there comes into manifestation Earth, the Principle of Stability and Solidity, or, which is the same thing, the stable or solid thing (*prithivi*).

Nor is there anything absurd in this statement;

for, as may be repeated once more, the sensation of the varieties of smell, as experienced
at this stage, is, as it were, all over the soul
and is as all-filling and overwhelming as any
others, and the consequent experience is as
great and mighty.

The Stages as Aspects of the Self

Thus from the experience of variation in
the five general objects of perception there
are produced also the five important factors
of the Physical, namely Ethereal Space (Akasha)
and the four others technically and symbolically
called Air (Vayu), Fire (Agni), Water (Ap),
and Earth (Prithivi). These ingredients are collectively designated in Sanskrit by the name
of *Bhutas*, i.e., the ever-passing Have-been's
(never the Are's), which are but Ghosts[48] of
the Real, the one ever-abiding Being that is
the inmost self of them all, as of the universe.

With the appearance of Earth (in the technical
sense) as the principle of Solidity, we have
reached the end of the process of Atman's
becoming limited and involved in various
grades of subjective and objective existence.

The Bhuta Earth is thus only Atman, the
Self, who has become limited and involved
to the uttermost degree and has ceased to
move. It is the lowest and most restricted

range of movements (*jagat*) of which the universe is made. In other words, Earth is only Atman that, having become a point, moves and waves within the greatest possible restriction, and acts as the odor-stimulating element in the universal structure.

Similarly it is only Atman who, having become so many points, appears as Water, Fire, and Air (all in the technical sense), moving and waving in ways and within ranges that are many and diverse.

Ethereal Akasha is, likewise, nothing but Atman stretching out, without a conceivable end, as an infinite number of firm, rigid lines which are the directions of Space—have indeed woven themselves into the fabric of Ethereal Space (*bhutakasha*)—and are, at the same time, upholders of things in their various positional relations.

Indeed, all the stages of Self-limitation on the part of Atman are, as already said, so many entities, inasmuch as they are only Atman involved in particular ways. And they all exist, as it were, simultaneously together from the Ultimate Being downward, or onward, to Earth.

Moreover, Atman appears not as one particle only of Earth or one entity only in each of the stages. On the contrary, the moment there beings a stage of the operation of space and time, which will be considered presently, there is produced in that stage a multiplicity of forms. Atman is inexhaustible and the process ceaseless. The one Atman, therefore, appears, in every stage where there are space-time conditions, ceaselessly in countless forms. This the Atman does in a manner which is somewhat like that of a single vital cell multiplying itself into countless numbers. These countless forms of Atman in the different planes react one upon the other and are inter-related in an infinite variety of ways. There is therefore no solipsistic isolation in any of the stages where there is the experience of Space and Time. There is no loneliness even where, as in the Ultimate Being, Space and Time are not. For loneliness has meaning only where there is limitation and a feeling of want. In any case, in every stage and plane where there is a space-time frame, there is also an inexhaustible number of individual souls, as there is in the physical world an exhaustless number of physical particles—Paramanus, ions, electrons, or whatever else may be the ultimate physical constituents; from the Vedic point of view, each is a Soul, a form of Atman, a Monad, but limited and restricted to the uttermost.

The Individual's Universe

If there is no solipsistic isolation in regard
to the experiencing subject, neither is there
one common universe of experience for all.
That is to say, each experiencing subject has
a universe which is absolutely and entirely
its own.[49] If, therefore, we speak of our really
different universes as one and the same—
when, for instance, we say "I am seeing the
same sun as you are"—that is only because
what is experienced is assumed to be similar.
The universe of John is the same as the universe
of James in exactly the same sense as the picture
seen by one eye is the same as that seen by
the other eye. It is a well-known fact that we
really see two different pictures with our
two eyes; but we think and speak of them as
one and the same picture because they are
similar and, as a rule, coalesce with each other.
Or, our different universes are one and the
same in the sense that a particular play acted
by one and the same dramatic company is
one and the same play for different groups
of people seeing it on different occasions.

That this is so needs little argument, once
we realize that each one of us really experiences what is primarily built up of our
own individual sensations, thoughts, and
ideas, even though these are induced in the

individual, in spheres of time and space, by the operation of what appears as outside, such as wave lengths and other stimulating movements. The idea may, however, be further illustrated in the following manner: Suppose two persons see before them a rod which appears to each to be, say, five feet long. In reality, it is quite possible that one sees it as a much longer rod than does the other, the eyes of the former having, let us say, a sort of magnifying power which is not possessed by the other. And if the two still speak of the rod as five feet long, it is because the foot-measure is seen proportionately elongated by the person with the magnifying eyes and the elongated measure is contained five times in the rod, exactly as the shorter measure, in the case of the second person, is contained the same number of times in the rod which the latter sees. Thus, while they may really see two different rods, they may yet speak of them as one and the same rod only because of the similarity, and even equality and constancy, of a certain relation subsisting between the rods experienced and the foot-measures, which, like the rods, are really different for the two different individuals. It is only in this sense of a certain similarity and constancy of relations that the universes experienced by different individuals are one and the same.

Thus it happens that if there is a multiplicity of experiencing entities as individuals, there is also a corresponding multiplicity of universes which are spoken of as the same by a sort of tacit convention.

Space and Time

This multiplicity of entities in the various stages is at once the cause and effect of what we experience as Space and Time. They begin to appear when multiplicity appears and Atman as subject begins to experience an object, or a series of objects, which, however, are only That One in another phase and seen in countless directions and in ceaseless succession. It is this experience of direction and succession which is the essence of Space and Time.

But Space and Time are not the same in all the stages, so that near and far, now and then, simultaneity and succession, cannot have the same meaning everywhere and under all conditions. In other words, Space and Time are uniform and obey uniformly the same sets of laws in relation only to a particular stage, say, the physical, but are totally different when experienced in relation to a different stage, for instance, the psychical. There is thus no absolute Space and no absolute Time, experienced in one uniform manner in all the stages of existence. Thus it is said that Space and Time as experienced by a Deva (a superhuman being, to be explained presently) are different from Space and Time as experienced by a human.

All of us can form some idea of this relativity of Space and Time from our common experiences in dreams as compared with experiences in the waking state. We may have dreams which would give us the idea of ranging over wide distances in space and of stretching across long years of time. But while thus dreaming we may not have slept for more than five minutes of time as experienced in waking life and not moved away even an inch of space as measured physically. But suppose we never woke up, and yet we had some means of knowing our experiences and comparing them with the experiences of a person who was, let us further suppose, keeping watch over us and was awake in physical space and time. Would we not then say that what are only the limited space of the room and five minutes of physical time to the waking one are, as it were, wide distances and long years to the sleeping person? We have to use the qualifying expression "as it were," because there can be no real comparison between the two sets of Space-Time experiences, the two Space-Time frames, which are really on two entirely different planes. Still, this would give us some idea of how Space-Time frames differ in different stages, so that one particular frame is true and uniform in relation only to a particular stage, plane, or set of experiences,[50] but not so when applied to a different plane.

*Siva. Bronze. South India. Vijayanager, 14th–
15th century. Asian Art Museum of San
Francisco, The Avery Brundage Collection.*

Part II

The Supreme Critic on the errors of the past and the present, and the only prophet of that which must be, is that great nature in which we rest as the earth lies in the soft arms of the atmosphere; that Unity, that Over-Soul, within which every man's particular being is contained and made one with all other; that common heart of which all sincere conversation is the worship, to which all right action is submission; that over-powering reality which confutes our tricks and talents, and constrains every one to pass for what he is, and to speak from his character and not from his tongue, and which evermore tends to pass into our thought and hand and become wisdom and virtue and power and beauty. We live in succession, in division, in parts, in particles. Meantime within man is the soul of the whole; the wise silence; the universal beauty, to which every part and particle is equally related; the eternal ONE. And this deep power in which we exist and whose beatitude is all accessible to us, is not only self-sufficing and perfect in every hour, but the act of seeing and the thing seen, the seer and the spectacle, the subject and the object, are one.

RALPH WALDO EMERSON, **The Over-Soul**

Part II

The universe produced from the one un-divided Atman by the on-rolling process of manifestation (*vivarta*) is thus a unified system, a mighty organism in which the inmost nucleus, the pervading Spirit and Self, is the one abiding Being, the one Supreme Person (Purusha) in the aspect of Brahman, the Word, as Isha, the Lord. Purusha ordains that every moving thing in this ever-moving universe —and all things are moving—shall yet move and dwell within ranges which are inexorably fixed and can be transgressed only at the risk of self-destruction as an individual entity. However, the ranges and limits can be so widened as to be coextensive with the whole universe—can even be entirely transcended by following a path of living, behavior, and action that is in harmony with the All, with the universal movement, with the Self and Spirit of the All.

Everything Is Alive

In this mighty living organism that is the Universe there is nothing really dead or absolutely unconscious. On the contrary, like every cell in a living, healthy body, every part and every thing in the universe is alive, though many parts are, as it were, in a comatose state; every part, every particle in it is ensouled, inspirited, by the All-aware, All-feeling Being that is Atman. What appears as dead and unconscious has the universal life and awareness in it as its inmost core, but completely cabined, cribbed, and confined—buried deep and as if in sound, dreamless sleep.

There is thus the Being of life, feeling and awareness, even in the most unfeeling stone, as in every single ion, in each electron, Anu, and Paramanu. And That One is there not in part, as a fragment, but in full, undivided being: there can be no division in the Being, no real limitation to THAT in Space, Time, or any other way.

This is beautifully illustrated in the story of Prahlada, even though that is found outside of the Vedas. We are told how, in order to rescue Prahlada from the heartless tortures inflicted by his wicked father, the Being Divine, in response to Prahlada's burning love for the Divine, appears in all the glory of That One from a crystal pillar in which, in all fullness, Divinity had remained hidden, deeply buried, as the inmost core of every particle in that cold, dead structure.

Part II

The Devas

This is why the Hindu maintains that the Vedic seers were telling nothing but simple, unvarnished truth when they declared that they perceived life and awareness in and behind every part and phenomenon of nature, visible and invisible, and called each manifestation a Deva, a divine flashing-forth from the one Central Being. The Devas, crudely and incorrectly interpreted as "gods," but more properly "angels,"[51] are thus no personifications of nature and its phenomena, but the very spirit and Self of the Universe seen through Nature's forms as through a prism. Indeed, it is to this day held in India that Nature and her phenomena, being but aspects of the one all-aware Being, can be consciously and feelingly communed with even now; and that the experiences of the ancient Rishi (Seer) can even today be, and indeed are, repeated by those duly qualified for the task. As a matter of fact, the Vedic worship performed even now, and three times a day, by Brahmans and others is a still living expression of this truth; so that when a Brahman offers his chant of ancient Vedic Words (Mantras) to the Sun or the Waters, he knows he is addressing himself really to the Spirit, to those aspects of the Being that are behind these physical forms of Nature, whether singly and collectively, whether as separate cells and monads, or as different groups of them constituting diverse organic wholes.[52] He knows, too, that he certainly is not worshiping phenomena that are really dead and are only personified in his imagination.

Indeed, from the Vedic point of view, the whole of Nature and the universe, visible or invisible, is much more than a living organism. It is a mighty hierarchy of living beings, superhuman, human, and subhuman. The subhuman is as obvious as the human, whereas the superhuman comprises, among others, Devas and human Souls that have attained ranges of awareness and movement surpassing those of ordinary beings.

At the head of this hierarchy stands the One who represents the first step taken by the Being starting on the path of self-limitation: Brahman, the Word, also named Isha, Ishvara, the Lord.

Brahman: The Beginning and Ending

From another point of view Brahman is the last product of the Universal Process (*vivarta*), being the final stage in the path backward, as it were homeward, to the Ultimate Being. For, once Atman has reached the stage of utmost limitation as in Earth (technical), THAT begins to retrace steps with a view to going back, ultimately, to the state of abiding Being in undimmed glory. The result is the gradual unfolding of Life and beings—living, conscious, self-conscious, and even super-conscious, transcending the self of the ego. In other words, the fruits of the endeavor to reach back to the Supreme Divine state of Being are germinal life, vegetable life, and then gradually human, superhuman, and angelic hosts, stretching onward toward Brahman. In this sense Brahman is the ultimate product of the process—a process of which only the second, the returning half, may be said to correspond, but partly, to what is now known as evolution, especially emergent evolution. As a process, emergent evolution undoubtedly means the unfolding of what already exists as something involved in previous stages, out of which it comes, so that its actual appearance is only an emerging.

The Worlds or Planes

The universe, as thus conceived, consists not only of beings that are living and intelligent, actually or potentially, but also of certain Grades, Planes, or Fields of Vision (*loka*), as they are called, i.e., worlds. These Planes are counted as either three or seven, depending on whether the last (or first) five are counted separately or taken together as one.

When counted as three the Planes (Lokas) are:

1. The Physical, or the Earth, corresponding to the human physical body (Bhur and Prithivi);

2. The Psychical, corresponding to what has been defined as the human soul, namely life (Prana), Concrete Mentality (Manas) including all the sense powers, and Ego (Ahamkara or Vijñana), behaving together as a unit (Bhuvas or Antariksha);

3. The Spiritual, corresponding to the human Mahat (Svar or Suvar, the Heavenly World).[53]

They are also counted as five, corresponding to what are called the "sheaths" or coverings (*kosha*) of Atman, the sheaths themselves being only the body and the other human factors regarded from a particular point of view. These Koshas or sheaths are:

1. The Physical (in this connection called Anna, "Food");

2. The Vital (Prana);

3. The Mental (Concrete Mentality, Manas);

4. The Ego (called Vijñana in this connection);

5. The Spirit, i.e., Mahat-Atman and Asat or Avyakta (in this connection called Ananda).

As the Koshas are five, the Lokas or planes related to them are, from this point of view, also the same number.

A Sacrifice of Joy

All this is produced by Purusha, the Supreme Person, who, as Atman, binds and sacrifices himself ceaselessly on the "cross of well-being" (*svastika*), pouring out his "life-blood" in unending streams of good will and love to the "four quarters" of space.[54] His is a sacrifice of joy, brought about by love (*ananda*), which of itself knows no bounds. To vary an ancient metaphor, forth from Purusha, in the act of ceaseless sacrifice, does the universe stream, an unceasing spring of joy that is ever at play on the space-time green in far-spreading, never-ending sprays.[55]

To use still another figure, the universe is a feast of love and joy in which Brahman is both the "food" and its "eater," both what is enjoyed and the enjoyer (the object and the subject). But as if the more to enjoy the food, to have the joy of eating it by countless mouths, Brahman spreads out in multifarious forms, so that each such form is a new mouth, a new aspect, with which to eat the food. Viewed in another way, this feast of love and joy spread by Brahman is enjoyed all the more by That One when shared with all creatures, even though they are but Brahman in diverse garbs.

And Atman has the joyous feast, and shares the enjoyment with all the beings that are the universal hierarchy, not once but countless times, from all eternity without a beginning. For, as already said, Atman goes on alternating, from beginningless time, between the two phases of Manifestation (*shrishti,* throwing out) and Absorption (*pralaya,* dissolution), so that, though there is the beginning of a particular universe, there is no absolute first start to the series of universes, which are all linked together as cause and effect.

Our Early Teachers

It thus happens that at no time in the history of a universe are beings constituting it exclusively of the lowest type. On the contrary, the first products in a new universe are beings of the loftiest character and widest possible range of experience. For when a universe passes away into dissolution, the results accomplished therein, the various beings produced at its different stages are not completely lost. There is absolutely no loss or waste of labor here, no energy destroyed. Rather all beings, as it were, fall asleep at their respective stations as Brahman falls asleep. And on a new universe coming into mani- festation, they all, as it were, wake up just when in the universal process that particular stage at which, in the previous universe, they had fallen asleep is again reached. There each being, as it were, merely resumes the march of life at the exact point where a halt had been called.

As it is the higher stages—the stages which are, as it were, nearest to Purusha—that reappear at the beginning and in the earlier life of the universe, the beings who wake up first are just those who had attained the greatest self-unfoldment in the past. They are the Sages, Seers, Rishis, and Prophets who bring over wisdom from across the gulf of ages and become teachers and guides, masters and kings, of those inferior to them in power and evolution, whether as products of a past uni- verse or of the new one. This is the reason why it is the universal tradition of all ancient peoples and civilizations that gods walked among humans in the earlier days, and that the first teachers and the founders of the arts and civilization were beings of a much higher order than ordinary humans: heroes, gods, and demigods, patesis and prophets, seers (Rishis), perfected beings (Siddhas), and fathers (Pitris).

This is also the reason why we find such lofty thoughts and ideas, such unexcelled royal and imperial power, pomp, and glory, such mighty lawgivers at the beginning of a racial development. And that is why, incidentally, the Vedas are not the babblings of an infant race, but contain wonderful wisdom, if properly understood. Of course, this does not mean that the whole Vedic literature in every part and detail is of the loftiest character. Besides being compilations of a mixed character, perhaps from the start, the Vedic texts are thousands of years old— the oldest literary records of Indian culture. As such they certainly have not come down to us absolutely unchanged or unmixed further with inferior material of later ages, even though the received texts have been preserved for at least three thousand years without undergoing any serious alterations. Nevertheless the fundamental ideas of the Vedas are of the loftiest character.

Even in parts supposed to be inferior and polytheistic (the latter perhaps the most absurd charge possible),[56] the Vedas are a way of describing nature and the universe viewed as a living organism, of which every part, every limb, even every cell—being but the one all-aware Atman veiled in various ways and degrees—can think, feel, and, as it were, talk. In much the same way in the opposite direction, science is a description of Nature and her workings, but looked upon as only mechanical movements of something dead and unintelligent. The Vedas are, in other words, the science of Nature and the universe conceived as an organic whole, as a living hierarchy—a science (*veda*) framed by superior beings from a past universe.

In any case, this is a view of things which need not be lightly set aside, especially as the other view, namely, of an unintelligent origin of things, cannot possibly be regarded as a definitely established fact. If, under the circumstances, the doctrine of an intelligent origin of the universe, as advocated by all schools of Vedic philosophy and most ancient schools of other peoples and practically all religions,[57] is accepted as truth, then there is no reason to doubt that the beings appearing at the earliest stages of our history are higher types developed in a past universe. Indeed there may come a time when this view of the origin of things will be fully accepted as the only rational one; and when or if this is done the philosophy of history as well as the whole of the early history of civilization will have to be rewritten.

In this new view, or rather the oldest view merely restated anew, progress will, of course, be recognized; but it will be progress like that in the education of a boy who has grown up into manhood. It is true, the boy has made progress in knowledge and experience; but it is also true that he has done so with the aid and cooperation of his teachers and elders who were already more advanced than he; and it would not be a correct account of his educational progress if the part that his teachers and elders played in it were left out. To give a complete history of the educational progress of the boy we must take note also of the help of the teachers. In the same way, if the Vedic point of view in regard to the origin of things be accepted, then we have also to admit that, in the progress of the universe and individuals therein, there has been no time when higher types of beings were not present helping and guiding the growth and development of types lower than themselves.

It is, however, not necessary that these higher types of beings, especially at the beginning, should always exist in the physical world. As a matter of fact such early teachers and guides and founders of civilization have often been regarded as superphysical entities. And it has been believed that even as superphysical entities they have inspired human beings, who have caught their ideas often as flashes of inspiration without knowing the sources from which they came.[58]

Beings from Past Universes

How the past is revived and the beings of a past universe wake up in a new one, and in what manner many of them do so with a full and detailed memory of the past, are topics which have been treated in many a text. One illustration of the process is to be found in the story of Vamadeva, who, it is recorded, began singing the song of his past memory immediately on waking up and proclaimed: "I once was Manu and again the Spirit of the Sun."[59] That beings can thus reappear from a past universe should not be difficult of comprehension for those who believe that they themselves will continue to exist as individual entities after death. For if they can thus endure as individuals in a bodiless condition, why cannot this be done by other beings, especially those who have attained states of development higher than those of average humanity, i.e., have grown stronger in character and reached wider ranges of experience? And the rationality and probable truth of the idea should be still less difficult of comprehension for those who accept reincarnation as a fact. For this reappearance of beings from a past universe is only a different application of the same principle that governs the rebirth of souls in this present universe of our own.

Karma

As a new birth of a soul in the present universe is governed by the law of cause and effect—the law of Karma, as it is called, the law of justice, of a perfect and absolute adjustment of things—so is the appearance of a new universe from a past one governed by the same moral law. In other words, the repeated appearance and disappearance of universes is governed by a law of absolute adjustment, of moral justice (*dharma*), which is thus the foundation on which the universe is built up.[60]

And the result which is aimed at by all this ceaseless activity and movement, this repeated appearance and disappearance of the universe, is the production of perfected beings, perfected in every respect, so that each of the final products shall be fully and completely divine and independent—all-knowing and all-powerful, each Brahman-like, each actually Brahman. But this final result is reached and an individual finally realizes the ultimate end, once and for all, only after long ages of countless births and deaths, not only in this physical world but also in other states of existence (*loka*).[61] The process is thus very slow indeed. It can, however, be accelerated by the method of self-training and self-realization known as yoga.[62]

Inner Knowledge

The earliest mention of yoga by name in the Vedic texts occurs in the Katha and Shvetasvatara Upanishads. Practically all the fundamental ideas of yoga, even as found in the later systematized and most authoritative treatise on the subject (the Yoga-sutras of Patanjali) are to be found—at least in a germinal form—in these two Upanishads, which both date back to a remote antiquity. It is, however, not necessary here to go into a detailed exposition of these texts on yoga. Only the main principles underlying the art need be set forth here; these are only a few and comparatively simple. They may be stated as follows:

The source of all knowledge and experience is really within our own inmost Self, who is also the ultimate Being.

Even in the most external of the states of experience, namely the physical, the only things which may be said to be outside are the stimulating movements or wave lengths. But these, too, are outside only under conditions of Space and Time as governing the physical, and, to a certain extent, the psychical spheres of experience. The moment, however, we touch in conscious experience the state of Universal Ideation (Mahat) or what has been called by some the Spirit, and thereby pass into a condition where Space and Time have a totally different significance—where they do not exist as dividing agents—at that very moment even the stimulating movements, the wave lengths, cease to be felt as anything external. Rather the sources of all such movements and waves are then discovered within—in oneself.

It thus happens that all knowledge—indeed all the universe, the whole "Kingdom of Heaven"—is literally within us; it is within us as eternal, timeless, spaceless, idealized objectivity lying in front of Atman, the eternal Subject and untiring Enjoyer.

For, though the Self within is felt to be smaller than the small (*anor aniyan*), that Self is, on the other hand, greater than the great (*mahato mahiyan*)[63]—greater than the earth, greater than the heaven, greater than the region between, greater than all the worlds. All active endeavor is That One, the Atman; all-desire, all-odor, all-taste is THAT; THAT is the fulfillment of all this. THAT is within the inmost heart.[64]

Within the heart is therefore "Ethereal

Space far extending as Ether and Space without. Within this, in truth, lie hidden both heaven and earth, both Fire and Air, both Sun and Moon, the lightning and the stars. Whatever else here in the external is and whatever is not—all that is hidden in this, in the heart."[65] All we need to do, therefore, is to tap this knowledge and experience within.

These are ideas which are not peculiar to the Vedas or to India; they have been experienced and uttered likewise by many in the Occident. Robert Browning, for instance, a poet belonging to a nation supposed to be the most matter-of-fact and practical, has expressed the thought in *Paracelsus* in the following vivid passage:

> Truth is within ourselves; it takes no rise
> From outward things, whate'er you may
>   believe.
> There is an inmost center in us all,
> Where truth abides in fullness; and around,
> Wall upon wall, the gross flesh hems it in,
> This perfect, clear perception—which is truth.
> A baffling and perverting carnal mesh
> Binds it, and makes all error: and to KNOW
> Rather consists in opening out a way
> Whence the imprisoned splendour may
>   escape,
> Than in effecting entry for a light
> Supposed to be without.

101

Concentrating on the Self

But if the whole Kingdom of Heaven is within and if all knowledge and all science are lying buried in our inmost self, how is it, then, that we do not always realize these in experience?

The obstacles in our way are only two, though caused in various ways, namely, dullness and distraction (*avarana* and *vikshepa*). Whenever persons endeavor, without full training and right preparation, to be silent and listen to the movement of the higher states of being within, to the Song Divine within, they either fall asleep, which is the effect of dullness, or their minds are distracted and wander, as it were, all over the universe. But if they can hold their consciousness in a tense state, keenly intent upon what is going on within the uttermost depth of their being, without either falling asleep or letting the mind wander, they will gradually but surely begin to be responsive to the subtlest throb, the most gentle whisper of Spirit, of the Self within. With constant practice, the whisper will grow into such loud tones and will swell into such volume that it will drown the whole universe.

The principle may be illustrated in the following manner. Let us suppose that there are strains of music coming to a man from some distance, being borne on the wind, and just audible at first as a faint note. Let us suppost further that our man concentrates his mind keenly and unwaveringly on that note, pouring out, as it were, his soul through the ears. It will be found that, as a result of this, the music that was at first heard as a very faint note has grown louder and louder till it has not only absorbed the man's entire attention and being, but has, as it were, filled the whole universe.

Or, take the classic instance of that master of archery, Arjuna, the Pandava prince, when, under the order of his teacher, he took aim at the eye of a bird sitting on a tree at a distance, and concentrated his soul on it. On being asked by the teacher what he was seeing at the time, Arjuna replied that he saw only the eye of the bird as filling the whole universe, and nothing else.

In some such way, by concentrating one's whole mind, soul, and consciousness on the Self within, one can be so fully conscious of THAT as to exclude all other movements of thought or feeling. But concentration of this character is impossible unless all dullness is entirely overcome and the mind and heart are freed from every distraction. The first step, therefore, is to be intensely active, so that idleness and laziness are entirely banished from life.

Two Ethical Codes

In the earlier stages of the soul's growth, when people are still undeveloped in character and strong individuality is lacking, they can maintain such an active life only, or at least chiefly, when prompted by selfish interests which are felt, at the time, as other than or opposed to the interests of their fellows. During these stages the code of moral behavior is what, in the Vedic view, is called "action with a personal desire" (*sakama karma*). The Vedas deliberately provide such a code in those parts technically known as *karma kanda*. In these desireful stages of growth (*sakama*), persons or nations would pray, for instance, that their own or their nation's enemies may be killed, that victory may be gained by their side. For such people the Vedas have prescribed the worship of and prayers to the Devas (angels, misinterpreted as gods), who are superhuman entities and have power to be of service to humans. The Vedas would regard it as an unspeakable blasphemy and sacrilege that selfish prayers of the character referred to should be addressed to the Ultimate Being or even to Brahman, the Word, who is not only the same and impartial to all, but is equally the core of every existence. For those of lower types, therefore, the Vedas have deliberately enacted selfish codes of conduct which are the only means to stimulate such people to activity and thus enable them to overcome dullness.

When, however, souls of this type, after millions of years of growth and countless embodiments, repeated births and deaths— innumerable reincarnations, in short—have gradually and laboriously developed a strong character and individuality, they soon discover that the very selfishness which has carried them so far, and which until then was very necessary, is now proving a great hindrance to further progress back to the divine home in the Ultimate Being whence they have strayed. For it is then seen how selfishness is the most potent and prolific cause of all passion and all disturbances of the mind—of distraction, the second great obstacle in the path of yoga.

When a soul has reached this stage of growth, then only is it ready for yoga proper, all previous endeavors and activities being but a prelude. This stage reached, we must find a way of still remaining intensely active— in order to be free from dullness—and must at the same time eliminate all causes of distraction, i.e., eliminate from heart and mind

105

all selfish notions and all thought of personal interests as separate from and opposed to the interests of others. For those are really not others, but only ourselves in different forms. In other words, we must change not so much our outward life, as our entire attitude, both toward what we may be doing and in our relations to the rest of the universe. We should and must adopt such an attitude as would enable us to engage in all necessary and useful activities without a selfish motive and without being so involved in the doings as not to be able to shake off thoughts of these activities whenever it is desired to do so.

The Moral Life

This art of doing things effectively and efficiently but without selfish motives and interests (technically "desire for fruit") and without being helplessly involved in them (technically "entanglement," *sanga*), is called *Karma Yoga* (Yoga of Action) and can be accomplished in various ways. The general principle is that, negatively, aspirants to the highest spiritual experience should refrain from thinking any thoughts, having any feelings and emotions, or doing any deeds which are likely to strengthen selfishness, i.e., the sense of separation; and that, positively, they should cultivate only such thoughts and feelings and practice only such deeds as will eliminate from the heart all selfishness and foster in it an abiding attitude and feeling of unity with every living thing and being—and all things are living. This is needed, moreover, because the realization in experience of the Being within and all that it implies is at the same time the realization in feeling of an absolute oneness with the whole universe and everything in it. Anything, therefore, which strengthens the feeling of separation (*bheda-buddhi*) from others, as selfishness does, is the most serious obstacle to the realization of the end sought by yoga.

In other words, the most essential foundation for yoga is *active moral* life of the very highest order possible. That is why Patanjali, the most authoritative expounder of the subject, first mentions moral discipline of the strictest and highest character, under the technical names of Yama and Niyama, and then lays down that the virtues to be cultivated by Yama and Niyama are the absolutely indispensable prerequisite for yoga. It is only after this that Patanjali speaks of the other steps of yoga. As a matter of fact, it is simply childish to talk of yoga unless the essential prerequisite in the shape of the highest moral life is first practiced and very largely developed.

Then only can one really walk the path of yoga.

The Upanishads are also most explicit on this point.[66] One of them (Isha) insists that devotees must never neglect their duties, which shall be done diligently, that they must not transgress the limits within which alone they can legitimately and fruitfully labor, and that they must rid themselves of all greed and selfishness. Another proclaims that those who have not refrained completely from evil behavior and have not the peace of heart and head—have not learned to hold their entire being absolutely tranquil (*samahita*)—cannot realize the ultimate Truth (Katha 2.24). The same Upanishad declares that those alone can attain the highest goal who have all their senses under perfect control and are ever alert in mind and ever pure in heart (Katha 3.8). In other words, aspirants to yoga must at once be active, alert in mind, and absolutely tranquil in heart, and must cultivate the feeling of love and oneness with all. This is the first step.

Physical Practices

Then there are conditions of the body which often greatly disturb the mind. The body therefore should be taken hold of as the second serious step—second not in sequence but as a matter of classification, so that its control is not to follow after first, but be simultaneous with the cultivation of the highest possible moral virtue and character. This is done by following certain physical and physiological practices of a very specific character, a regimen which undoubtedly gives persons not only a complete mastery over the nervous and muscular systems of the body, but enables them to keep it in a perfect state of health.[67]

The Final Goal

Next there is a third group of practices which are purely mental, leading up to what is called *Samadhi,* which is, in its ultimate form, the state of awareness of the own true being of the Atman,[68] absolutely free from and independent of all relations to any objectivity, which has vanished away. This is also the Nirvana of the Buddha, the unlimited Awareness (*anantam vijnanam*) without any relation to Earth and Water, Fire and Air, i.e., all objectivity, which has vanished from its view (see Kevaddha Sutta, end). Nirvana is described in exactly the same terms as applied to Brahman-Atman in the Vedas, such as unborn, uncompounded, eternal, and the like.

This is the final goal; when this is realized,

everything else is heard and seen, everything enjoyed, life fulfilled to the uttermost. This is the final answer to the question which, thousands of years ago, Shaunaka asked of Angiras, saying: "On what being by experience known, O master, is all this [i.e., the universe] experienced and known?"[69]

This goal can be realized gradually, through various stages and only when we are perfect in yoga; and this again is possible only when what we appropriate from the universe, as physical, mental, and spiritual food, is so appropriated that the act can serve only to purify our entire being as an individual, by establishing the most complete, the most perfect harmony between ourselves and the All. When our being is thus purified, there arises before us the firm, imperishable memory of our past existences, our countless births and deaths during millions of years covering many a world-period of Manifestation and Dissolution (*shrishti* and *pralaya*) during which we have lived as an individual. This memory is imperishable because nothing, not even a jot or tittle of our experience, is lost. The fruits of all remain deeply buried in the unconscious strata of our being and now rise up before the perfected individual in full recollection.[70]

When this is accomplished, then only can

the fetter of individuality—the illusory ego, forged with the links of experiences stretching far and away into the remotest past (only now remembered as a single whole)—be broken forever and the aspect of Atman so long kept chained by that particular individuality set completely free.[71]

Atman, thus set free from all limiting individuality and all relations to qualifying objectivity, is then one with the Ultimate Being; or, more accurately, has now the realization, in awareness and feeling, of the oneness which, though existing always, has hitherto remained, as it were, quite forgotten and unnoticed. The perfect realization of this oneness of one's inmost and utmost Self with the Ultimate Being is the experience of what is called objectless Samadhi, that state of awareness, mentioned above, from before which all objects have entirely vanished (*nirvikalpa-samadhi*).

A New View

But when yogis, as it were, descend from this state of transcendent objectless experience —that is, the state of supreme ecstatic vision— or, as it is also said, though incorrectly, "wake up" to a consciousness of objects as things outside, they enjoy and experience everything, all objectivity, the whole universe in the same way as Brahman does.[72]

In other words, when they "wake up" to objective life again from objectless experience, the universe changes its aspect completely. It is an experience which is comparable, though in a very faint manner, to the experience of change which the world undergoes in the eyes of one who is truly, "madly," in love.

The idea may perhaps be made a little clearer in another way. Suppose the findings of physics in regard to the ultimate nature of matter are true, representing actual, objective facts. Suppose, in other words, that a physical object, say a table, is actually composed of ions and electrons, moving round nuclei, with inter-spaces between. Suppose, further, that some people have developed the power of vision to such an extent that their eyes are able to magnify things immeasurably and see the ions and electrons composing the table. Now it is obvious that such people looking at the table, will no longer see what they saw before, or what others may be seeing now. On the contrary, instead of seeing the table of familiar experience, they would perceive now the "second" table of Eddington, consisting only of wave lengths and the like. In other words, what they would actually be seeing now would not be a table at all, but a whirling mass of ions and electrons. The table of familiar experience has for them vanished, and in its place they see only a mass of points executing all kinds of beautiful movements.

In some such way the universe of previous experience vanishes from before those who have realized Samadhi; what they experience as the universe when they "wake up" from Samadhi is a very different thing, is only the "vibrating thought" of Brahman as life pulsating through all Space and Time; and they feel themselves to be one with that life and therefore with the whole universe as now seen.

Being one with all, they know and experience all; nothing is beyond their reach, nothing can remain hidden from their gaze; they have become all-knowing at will. "In himself he now sees all things and beings, equally as he sees himself in all things and beings."

For such seers, life's uttermost purpose is fulfilled. Whatever wish or desire they now have, they find satisfied at once: only they have no personal desires now, no interests which are opposed to the interests of the whole; such desires and such interests were left behind long before they reached the spiritual heights where they now habitually dwell.

Natural Virtue

The result is that righteousness is now a habit with such beings, no longer a virtue inasmuch as it is no longer an effort, a striving. Virtue is now their native nature: hitherto covered up with ignorance (*avidya*), with the illusory notion and feeling of a separate ego, an individual I, this natural state now shines out in its native glory. These enlightened ones cannot but be righteous, any more than fire can be anything but hot and burning. Hence they have now transcended all such conceptions as vice and virtue, which have meaning only insofar as we have an "evil nature," or rather, evil propensities to contend with, and individual, separate desires and wills and interests to fulfill. They are now above all such thoughts and feelings, and therefore above all good and evil. Such beings are the absolute good—if that conveys any meaning.[73]

Those who are "awake" are all-loving, despising none. They cannot help it, because all are parts of themselves in conscious feeling and experience—all things and beings are only themselves in diverse forms; as Brahman, "all-knowing and all things he becomes; he sees himself in all and all in himself."

Part II

These beings are fearless. Whom can they fear? Others are but aspects of themselves. They are not the body, which, as body, they now feel to be no more than the clothes they may be wearing. They have no personal and separate interests, no individual possessions, power, name, fame, and reputation. They can therefore have no fear of injury to any of these by anyone. They are Brahman in conscious experience—the heart and soul and spirit, the inmost Self of every thing and being. They are the inmost Self even of the Angels (Devas), who are now subject to their will and they to the will of none. They are therefore utterly fearless.

Such ones are conquering heroes, having triumphed over all sorrow and suffering and all privations that limited life is heir to. They have the power to prevent any suffering coming to themselves. But they do not run away from an occasion or a circumstance that may be the cause of suffering, that may affect or injure the body and whatever may pertain to it. They have no desire to run away from these, for they know that such occasions for injury or destruction to the body can arise only in payment of the last remnants of moral and spiritual obligations (*karma*) incurred in the past on account of the now transcended individuality.[74]

Perfected Beings

Thus live those who have realized themselves fully and experienced the ultimate Self as one with the Self of all the Universe. Pure and soft as a lily, and yet strong and fearless, loving and joyous, they continue life on earth, singing, as it were, the song of triumph and of oneness with all things and beings.[75]

But joyous and happy as they are and free from every obligation of life, these perfected beings of transcendent experience are never idle. On the contrary, they—the "Great Ones (*mahantas*), full of Peace, saintly—live and work, without noise, naturally, like the season of Spring that, unobserved, makes all of Nature smile with joy. They have themselves crossed over to the other side of the fearful ocean of repeated births and deaths, and they help others to cross it without seeking a reward."[76]

When such great souls of Divine Freedom cannot, or are not required to, be of service in any specific manner, it is held that they are even then of the greatest service to humankind by their very presence with us.

Then, when all duties are done and all obligations of the past are paid back and the time comes for them to discard the mortal coil, as they say, they often do so by an act of the will.[77] The body discarded, they are pure unblemished Brahman, one with THAT and yet somehow, as it were, a different center whence may well up a new universe of love and joy: a new singer of a fresh universal song.

In Christian phraseology such liberated ones have resurrected themselves and risen from the rock-bound tomb of matter and materiality, from all Negation; neither can they "die any more," not being compelled to be born any more. They have become not only "equal unto the angels," but greater than they—indeed, the angels' inmost and controlling self.[78]

Perfected beings have become, as it were, new creators, as they have reached everywhere, pure and shining, bodiless, without disease, one with Awareness that needs no instrument of bodily nerves, untouched by evil. For all eternity they have now become the dispensers of the joys, even of the sorrows, of life to beings not yet returned to the divine home, dispensing joy and sorrow according to the various deserts, as is right and just.[79]

Such is the end, such the consummation of human life in the Vedic view.

Epilogue

The following benediction in the words of the great Hindu poet and dramatist Kalidasa[80] forms a beautifully conceived epitome—and may thus be regarded as a fitting conclusion —of the sublime outlook on life that is set forth in the foregoing pages:

Vedanteshu yam ahur Eka-Purusham vyapya sthitam rodasi yasminn Ishvara-ity ananyavishayah shabdo yatharthaksharah antar yash ca mumukshubhir niyamita-pranadibhir mrigyate sa sthanuh sthira-bhakti-yoga-sulabho nihshreyasayastu vah.

This may be interpretatively rendered into English as follows:

May He whom in the "Veda-Ends"[81] they call the one, the only true Person, established firm, pervading the "ever-roaring twins"[82] [of Life's straight and curving lines[83] that are the warp and woof of heaven and earth and all];

In whom the sonance Lord, unmeaning elsewhere, doth find its true significance;

Who is sought within their inmost soul, by those desiring Freedom, with all movings

119

of life, thought, and passions hushed
and controlled;
Who yet is easy to attain by the art of un-
shaking, all-forgetting love[84]—may He,
the unmoving Pillar of all that moves and
lives, be unto your attaining That which
is the Unsurpassable Good, the Supreme
Worth.[85]

Notes

Part I

1. Cf. R. D. Ranade, *A constructive survey of Upanishadic philosophy* (Poona, 1926), esp. chap. 4, "Roots of later philosophies." See also Deussen, *The Philosophy of the Upanishads* (Edinburgh, 1906) and the first volume of his *Allgemeine Geschichte der Philosophie* (2d ed., Leipzig, 1907), dealing with the philosophy of the Mantra part of the Vedas; S. Radhakrishnan, *Philosophy of the Upanishads* (London, 1924).
2. *Ishavasyam idam sarvam yat kim ca jagatyam jagat* (White Yajur-Veda 40.1—Isha *Upanishad* 1).
3. Cf *na'nyah pantha vidyate 'yanaya,* Shvet. Up. 6.15.
4. Cf. *tad dhavato 'nyan atyeti tishthat* and *nainad deva apnuvan purvam arshat* (Isha Upanishad 4).
5. That *ananda* means also "love" will be clear if we recall that the word is sometimes rendered by *priti,* and is, in one form of its manifestation in the individual, sexual pleasure, the function of *upasthendriya.* Cf. also Brih. Up. 4.3.21, where the supreme and final experience of realizing Brahman is likened to the feeling of being embraced by the beloved woman and of forgetfulness of all else in that enjoyment. The feeling of *ananda* is further described as *svarupa-vishranti,* absolute rest in oneself, that is to say, *ananda* is peace.
6. On this point, see the writer's *Kashmir Shaivaism.*

Avidya is really "negation" (*nishedha*) of Being, while *tamas* is "contraction" (*samkocana*).

7. The word *brahman* is neuter only in form, not in meaning, in the same way as for instance, *mitra*, "friend," is neuter, *darah*, "wife," is masculine plural, and *kalatra*, "wife," is neuter, only in form. Such expressions should be translated in reference to their meaning and not according to their grammatical gender in Sanskrit. It is absurd to refer to Brahman, the all-intelligent, all-bliss, and ever-abiding Being, by the pronoun *it*, as though something unintelligent and unfeeling. This has been the cause of a great deal of misunderstanding as to what is really meant by Brahman, who is, in strict truth, neither male nor female, and certainly not an unintelligent neuter entity such a stone, any more than the real personality of a human being is either male, female, or neuter. Brahman is derived from the root *brih*, "to grow, to grow great," which is undoubtedly only *vridh* in another form. If so, the English "Word" is ultimately the same as the Vedic Brahman even etymologically.

8. But literally perhaps "what spreads thread-like or net-like" all over the universe and thus controls everything in it; Ishvara is described as *jala-vat*, "the net-wielder" or "made up of nets." The technical names *sutratman*, "the Atman that spreads thread-like," and *antaryamin*, "the puller from within," may also be compared in this connection.

9. See footnote 5 above for the meaning of *ananda*.

10. The term *kalpa* is used also in the sense of a

complete cycle of one phase of manifestation and one phase of potentiality.

11. The state of potentiality is therefore referred to as *salila,* "the ever-moving water," *maho-arnas,* "the great flood," and *samudra arnava,* "the ocean in the flow." In the Puranas it is called *karana-samudra* or *karana-vari,* "ocean of causes." In the Sankhya it is Prakriti in the *pralaya* state in which there is but a *sadrisha-parinama,* i.e., homogeneous movement, a gentle internal but waveless flow, as there may be in an ocean. Prakriti, which is really a "process," is always moving, never at rest. Only, when it appears as the actual universe it is still flowing, but, as it were, in a threefold current, giving rise to all kinds of eddies, ripples, and waves, which are the diversified objects. But in *pralaya,* when there is only the *sadrisha-parinama,* there is but a uniform flow without any waves and ripples whatsoever.

May not this be the primeval Water of Thales? And may not the name *Thales* be a play on "sea"?

12. RV. 10. 129.2: *anid avatam svadhaya tad ekam,* lit. "breathed windless, by his own power, That One." The word *svadha* is important. It means really what is called *svabhava, maya,* and *prakriti* in later writings.

13. The term *prana* is usually rendered "breathing"; this, however, is only a function of *prana.*

14. For the probable derivation and literal meaning of *akasha,* see below.

15. On this point, see the writer's *Kashmir Shaivaism.* The name *akasha* itself probably conveyed this idea originally, being most probably derived

from a = *samantat,* "in all directions," and *kasha,* "reed" or what looks like reeds. In various Vedic texts the universe is referred to as *yajna,* "sacrifice," which then is figured as something woven, as with threads. Cf. also the epithet *jalavat,* applied to Isha, and the term *sutratman,* both mentioned above.

16. On this point, see the writer's *Hindu Realism* (section on Paramanus).

17. For an explanation of the idea of Akasha being the basis and medium of sound, see the writer's *Hindu Realism* (section on Akasha).

18. The act of taking such things into the body is partly the function of *hastendriya* (Power of Handling) and partly of *prana* (Vitality).

19. On this point see the writer's *Kashmir Shaivaism.*

20. Manas has as its function *samkalpa* and *vikalpa,* besides *vyavaccheda.*

21. The question of the origin of things abstract can never be finally decided for everybody by merely inferential reasoning. Inferentially, the abstract will be always regarded by some as things produced and built up gradually from elements supplied by experiences of the concrete; while others will hold, equally rationally, that abstract things are latent, innate in us, and that the experiences of the concrete only provide the occasion for their coming out into play. Speculative or inferential reasoning by itself can never satisfy all persons equally in regard to any question, even when they are equally intellectual. There will always be Deweys and Bertrand Russells, Eddingtons and Whiteheads, who will never all agree fully on any question on merely inferential grounds.

Naisha tarkena matir apaneya, "By mere argument this truth [about the transcendental] cannot be reached." The function of what in India corresponds to the philosophy of the Occident is not, therefore, to *discover* truth of the abstract and the transcendental, but only to discuss the rationality or otherwise of what is *given* as statements embodying positive experiences of the transcendental (only *vicara* on what is given as *shruti*). For it is held in India that all transcendental truth, no matter how abstract, can be directly and positively experienced by duly qualified persons by means of yoga (of the right kind, of course). (The Vedanta-sutra equivalent of *naisha tarkena matir apaneya,* Katha 2.9, is *tarkapratishthanat,* Vedantasutras 2.1.11.)

22. This is also the *vijñana* (one of the five Skandhas) of Buddhist philosophy. In the Katha Upanishad it is referred to by the additional names of *jñana-atman,* i.e., Atman of limited individual experience, and *buddhi,* Intelligence and Reason. The term *buddhi,* however, is used in the Sankhya as an alternative name for *mahat,* to be considered next. The Sankhya use of *buddhi* as a technical term is the more usual practice.

23. This numbering is, of course, only according to one particular method of classification. The stages are greater or less in number according as several intermediate stages are counted as independent ones or not. In the Taittiriya Upanishad, for instance, the Bhutas are declared at once as coming out of Atman without a mention of any of the antecedent stages in the process.

125

It may be noted here that the scheme of Buddhist Nidanas, twelve in number ("Causal Nexus") is only another way of presenting the same process (see the writer's *Great Origination*). The later attempts, Ceylonese and otherwise, to interpret the Nidanas without reference to the antecedent and closely allied Upanishadic and Sankhya thought have resulted in almost childish absurdities. The Buddha repeatedly declared that he only reproclaimed the ancient "Arya Dharma." Only the garb was somewhat new—not completely. In the case of the Nidanas, several of them are identical even in name with some of the stages named above; while others are easily recognizable as identical in meaning, though differing in names. The Nidanas are twelve in number because the Buddha counts certain intermediate stages as independent ones, between the Indriyas with Manas (taken together as *Shad-Ayatanas*) and the Physical, while he leaves out Prana and includes *Bhuta-matras* in Nama-Rupa.

The chief difficulty lies in the supposed denial by the Buddha of an abiding, timeless and spaceless, ultimate Being. But let such doubters read carefully the epithets used by the Buddha to describe Nirvana; they will then see that Nirvana *is* this ultimate Being—Nirvana being spoken of as Deathless (*amrita*), Bliss (*sukha*) and Endless Awareness (*anantam vijnanam*), Unborn (*ajata*), Uncreate (*akrita*), and Uncompounded (*asamskrita*).

Nirvana is the background of all experience;

except for Nirvana there would be no experience at all, declares the Buddha, and no escape from limited experience. See the statement on Nirvana attributed to him in the Udana (8.1 and 3).

The other difficulty in establishing the true relation between the teachings of the Buddha and of the Veda is the equally supposed notion that the Buddha denied continuity of the individual after death. As a matter of fact the Buddha's teaching in this respect is identical with the Vedantic, namely continuity of identity in the midst of ceaseless change. Because of this only, one could call back to memory, according to both Buddhism and Vedic Philosophy, all the details of one's past existences during thousands, even millions, of years.

As for the Vedic Devas, the so-called "gods," the Buddha declared he was seeing them always and everywhere, even though invisible to most other people; and Buddhists, even of Ceylon, pray to them every day of their lives, as they make daily offerings to the Buddha. Compare the daily prayer of the Ceylonese and other Southern Buddhists not only to gods of the sky and earth, but also to Nagas and other unseen entities (*akashattha ca bhummattha naga deva mahiddhika*); Vishnu is the presiding deity in many a Buddhist monastery and temple. (Notice, for instance, the painted figure of Vishnu immediately on entering the Shrine of the Buddhist Vihara built a few years ago in Calcutta by Anagarika Dharmapala, of Ceylon.)

In fact there is not a statement attributed to the Buddha in the whole of the Pali Suttas— supposed to be the oldest record of Buddhist teachings—which goes against any of the fundamental ideas of the Vedic Philosophy. Buddha denounces only the abuses, wrong values and interpretations read into the Vedas. But so does the Bhagavad-Gita, a most orthodox and authoritative work on the Vedanta. Even the Upanishads, themselves parts of the Veda, regard large sections of it as inferior (*apara*).

24. For a fuller statement of this process, see the writer's *Kashmir Shaivaism*.

25. What is called *avidya* is only the experience "nothing is known" (*na vidyate kim api*), which again is the same as "nothing is." Thus *avidya* is the equivalent of *asat*.

26. This visioning stage is therefore called *pashyanti* in schools of tradition other than the Vedic.

27. From this point of view they correspond to some of the nine *Sattavasas* of the Buddhist teaching.

28. The dominant mood at this stage is *eshana*, "seeking," desiring, willing; and what is found by seeking is *artha*, "thing desired and sought."

29. It should be noted that the term *prana* is used in a twofold sense, both to signify life in general and as the name of a particular function of it.

30. See Prashna Upanishad 3.6.

31. Cf. Prashna Upanishad 4.4: *ahar ahar Brahma gamayati*.

32. Compare the Christ-experience, "I and my Father are one."

33. Cf. Prashna Upanishad 3.7-12.
34. Cf. the *prathama spanda*, the first vibrating movement of Shiva Tattva in Trika Philosophy. Compare also the Gospel of John, 1.3-4, where life is identified with the Word. Life is a "waving" movement, like that of the flutter of a flag in the wind. Compare Rig-Veda 1.1.10 and note the play therein on *ketu* and *chit* and *dhi.*
35. Cf. Prashna Upanishad 3.3.
36. Compare the "death-at-will" of Bhishma. Several cases are quoted even in modern times as examples of "death-at-will" by simply withdrawing life from the body by an act of Manas.
37. In none of the Vedic texts proper is this last step clearly explained, nor even any suggestion given, as in most of the other steps explained above, as to how the Bhutas appear from the Bhuta-matras, unless we take as such a suggestion the *trivritkarana* of Chandogya Upanishad 6.3.3-4, which is a foreshadowing of the *pancikarana* idea. But the interpretation given here is traditional and quite old, and in this sense authentic.
38. Sanskrit *kosha* or *kancuka*.
39. It is actually symbolized by a monkey in the Buddhist scheme of the Nidanas, in which it corresponds to *vijñana* as a *Skandha.*
40. Tamas, Sattva, and Rajas are spoken of in Vedic texts respectively as black (blue), white, and red (*Shvetashvatara* Up. 4.5) and also by another figure, as food (*anna*), water (*ap*), and light (*tejas*) (Chandogya Up. 6.4), and are later symbolized respectively (a) by blue in the throat of Shiva, who as destroyer of the universe

is the embodiment of Tamas; (b) by the wheel-disk and wheeling Eagle (*garuda*) of Vishnu, who is the chief embodiment of Sattva; and (c) by the four faces—uttering forth words of creation in the four directions (meaning all directions) of Space—of the red Brahma, who is the embodiment of Rajas. The names Tamas (Darkness), Sattva (Existence), and Rajas (Flaring up) are very significant and appropriate. It is obvious how the suppression of the All into Nothingness producing darkness, as it were, and the scattering around of everything into dust and thin air, as it were, are appropriately called Tamas and Rajas. The wheeling tendency is called Sattva, Existence, because, left to themselves, Rajas would scatter everything into atoms and ions, and Tamas would compress everything into Nothing. That is to say, by itself neither Rajas nor Tamas could keep anything existing as such a thing. It is the third tendency which, by whirling things round ceaselessly within limited orbits—whether members of the solar system or particles constituting tiniest atoms—keeps them existing (in Sanskrit, *sat*)—whence the tendency is Sattva, "be-ness." This is undoubtedly the reason why *vartamana*, literally whirling, means "existing," "present."

Tamas, Sattva, and Rajas—or, as they are generally enumerated in later literature, Sattva, Rajas, and Tamas—are the famous Gunas, literally threads or strands which weave themselves into attributes of things or, in other words, into the things themselves. They are the threads with which is woven the net that the Lord (Isha) wields (*jalavat*). For a fuller account of the Gunas see the writer's *Kashmir Shaivaism*.

41. This need not startle anyone in the Occident in view of the fact that even scientific thinking, as represented, for instance, by such a distinguished physicist and astronomer as Professor Eddington, is coming to realize that the universe is built up of "mind-stuff" and that the so-called "matter" is only "mind" in another shape, and produced from "mind"— "such stuff as dreams are made on."

42. See the writer's *Hindu Realism*, pp. 54-61.

43. That the *dishah* are the essence of Ethereal Space and inseparably connected with "hearing," which has again no meaning without reference to sound, is to be found repeatedly mentioned in the Upanishads.

The figure of cloth or of something woven, as applied to Ethereal Space, and indeed to the whole universe, conceived as *yajña*, "sacrifice" (to be explained later), is also often met with in Vedic texts.

One of the alternative names for Akasha, Ethereal Space, is *vyoman*, which is derived from *ve* or *va*, "weaving," with the prefix *vi*, "diversely," and thus means literally "webbing," the significance of which will now be understood. Because *vyoman*, Ethereal Space, is literally a webbing of lines, living though imaginary (*dishah*), like spreading-out (*a*) reeds (*kasha*), going everywhere and then turning back and coiling round like matted locks of hair which Shiva the Benign Lord wears, he is spoken of as *vyoma-kesha,* "space-haired." Slightly varying the figure, it is only the straight-going aspects of the lines which are likened to his hair, while their curving and coiling aspects are spoken of as the divine life-giving stream of Ganga (the heavenly Ganges), meandering through the hair. Each of the straight lines is also symbolized as a *Linga* of which no limit can be found; neither Brahma nor Vishnu—one going upward and another downward ceaselessly for ages—could ever come to the Linga's end. The coilings are in that case pictured as serpents twining round the Linga. One other symbolism is that of Ganga issuing from Vishnu's feet, or highest path (*parama pada*), as from a spring of honey (*madhu-utsa*). There are numerous other forms of symbolism representing this conception of Akasha as a webbing of straight and curved lines of living energy.

44. Characterized in an old stanza as *dikkaladyana-vacchinnanantacinmatramurti.*

45. That the all-upholding *dishah,* spreading everywhere, are Lines of Force and weave themselves into the Ether or Ethereal Space need not be an absurd idea. The theories of physics tend to do away with the conception of the ether as a "jelly-like" substance. And science may find that there may still be something like the ether, but made up of lines of force, as the Vedic conception has it.

46. The Sanskrit word *rupa* means both color and form, as well as beauty.

47. Cf. *yat kathinam sa prithivi* (Shariraka Upanishad).
48. The word *bhuta* means both "ghost" and "what has been."
49. In technical language, universes, like the experiences of them, are *pratisvika*, "each one's own."
50. This ancient idea of the relativity of space and time based on experience and justifiable purely on psychological grounds may be compared with Einstein's Theory of Relativity based on mathematical reasoning.

Part II

51. Probably identical etymologically with *angiras*, which is often used as an epithet of Devas.
52. Thus from the Vedic point of view there is more truth in what is despisingly called "animism" than in the theory of an unfeeling and unintelligent Nature, i.e., the theory of materialism advanced by scientists and their followers in the last century, though discarded now by at least a number of distinguished scientists.
53. Cf. the oft-repeated expression *svarge loke mahiyate*, and note the play on *mahiyate*, the suggestion of Mahat. In the sevenfold division, Svar is what corresponds to ego taken by itself, and the next Loka, Mahas, is the one corresponding to Mahat. The Lokas transcending Mahas in the sevenfold counting are Jana, Tapas, and Satya. They correspond to states of experience which, it is maintained, can be had only by yoga. They are not easily distinguishable intellectually and hence are

generally not mentioned in theoretical studies. In the Trika Philosophy, however, their subjective correspondences are well recognized in the Tattvas transcending what is called "Purusha," which name is given in that system to a conditioned aspect of the ultimate Being. All these lokas are daily meditated on in the Vedic worship as it is now practiced in the form of Samdhya by means of the famous Gayatri. They are then regarded as only the objective effulgence (*bhargas*) of the ultimate Being conceived as Savitri, who is at the same time sought to be realized subjectively as our inmost self, stimulating all thoughts within us.

54. The meaning of the cross and sacrifice by crucifixion, and of the crucifixion of Christ, as conceived by yogis, will be discussed in a subsequent essay.

55. Cf. *sphuranti shikara yasmad anandasyambare 'vanau,* "from whom are blossoming forth sprays of love and joy in heaven and earth" (Yogavasishtha).

56. The Vedas are no more polytheistic than they are, to coin a new word, "polyanthropoistic." The so-called gods of the Vedas have no more independent and separate existences than humans have: both humans and gods are equally so many different manifestations of the only reality, Brahman, who is the one God, if "God" must be used. It is so absurd to call the Vedas polytheistic that Max Müller was obliged to coin a new term, "henotheism," for the Vedic conception of the Devas.

57. The doctrines of an intelligent origin of things

are chiefly of two types. One of these is represented by the religions of Semitic origin which believe in a God like a mighty king, like a "Caesar," as Prof. A. N. Whitehead has it. This God, according to such religions, is the creator of everything. But this God, too, can create, even at the beginning of the universe, the highest types of beings. As a matter of fact, it is the belief of such religions that this is so. The second type of doctrine of the intelligent origin of the universe is what we have explained above as the Vedic view. Substantially, this is the view also of Buddhism and Jainism, both of which, along with Brahmanism, hold that the present universe is only one in a beginningless series, reappearing and disappearing from time to time.

58. It was the daily practice of the Buddha, we are told in the Pali books, to wake up, like all spiritual people in India, in that early hour before the dawn known as *brahmamuhurta*, when, in the beautiful words of J. S. Hoyland, quoted by Professor Eddington (*Science and the Unseen World*, pp. 44-55) the veil between the seen and the unseen seems to be thinnest. He would then survey the world with his "divine Buddha eye" and pick out those who were ready for spiritual guidance and then send out to them his thoughts, which would be received by the persons so selected often as inspirations, but coming as though from within themselves. It is in this way, the followers of the Vedas hold, that we are often inspired by unseen entities; some of them may have

physical existences but at a distance or out of sight, while others are entirely superphysical.

59. This occurs first in Rig-Veda 4.26 and is quoted in Brih. Up. 1.4.10. In the latter passage it is explained by certain commentators as referring to the recovery of the past memory by Vamadeva on the realization of Brahman. But the section is one dealing with the origin of things at the beginning of a new world-period and it is therefore more logical to take the Rig-Vedic mantra quoted therein as illustrating the recollection, in a new universe, of the memory of things in a previous one. The passage in the Upanishad really means: "Whoever of the Devas woke up (at the beginning of a *kalpa*) he became the same as he was before, and that was the case with whoever woke up of the Rishis and of men." This means that these also, like the Devas (angels), again occupy their respective stations, similar to those in a previous universe.

60. On this subject see the writer's *Hindu Realism*.

61. For a fuller exposition of the doctrine of reincarnation consult the writer's *Hindu Realism*.

62. Etymologically the same word as "yoke," meaning "yoking" or "harnessing," i.e., disciplining oneself.

63. Katha Upanishad 2.20.

64. See Chandogya Upanishad 3.14.2-4.

65. Chandogya Upanishad 8.1.3. The meaning of all things existing together in a timeless state is not that this is a mere collection of things as we know them through the physical senses in physical space and time. They exist as a

general and universal synthesis; this is very different from a mere aggregate, from which the synthetic ideal state differs as much as an ideal triangle, i.e., triangularity, differs from a mere aggregate of triangles of various shapes and dimensions.

66. It is surprising and incomprehensible that some people should prattle about the Vedic attitude as less ethical than certain others. The Vedic people and literature produced a Vajashravasa who gave his son over to Death because of a word given casually; a Harischchandra who gave away a whole kingdom and would make a gift of his own body because of a promise to give away everything, though the promise was made on a misunderstanding; a Bhishma who would not swerve even by an inch from his determined course in carrying out a given troth, even when he had every opportunity and every temptation to do so, and who remained a bachelor and only a king-maker instead of a king, which he could easily have been so many times; a Yudhishthira who was made to see Hell because he only slightly prevaricated and swerved from the truth and even that only when the Divine tempted him to do so (he would be no great character if he yielded to the temptation at the instigation of any lesser being); a Ramachandra who put away his dearly beloved consort in order to carry out his kingly duties as he conceived them (perhaps mistakenly, as some would say), and would not take another in her place even though required to do so for purposes of

religious rites, but had a golden image of the Queen made to serve the religious need; a Sita and a Savitri, noblest examples of female chastity and devotion. A people and literature that could produce these and many similar characters, and have not ceased doing so even now, knew and know the value of moral life and ethics far better than do most of their critics. One feels almost tempted to hurl back at such critics the cutting words of Kalidasa: *paratisamdhanam adhiyate yair vidyeti e santu kilaptavacah* (Shakuntala 5.25).

67. There are yogis who maintain that—following the principle that underlies the qualifying clause "if it be possible" in Jesus' prayer to take away from him the "cup" of crucifixion— all things may be possible, but it is not always right, or in Christian phraseology, is not in accordance with the "will of God," to do all things or get all things done. In the phraseology of the philosophy based on the Vedic view, we should not run away from Prarabdha Karma (to be explained later), but must face it. It is on this principle that yogis often allow themselves to suffer bodily torture, whether from disease or in other ways, even when they could easily prevent it. They do this, it is held, not only on their own account—to meet their own Prarabdha—but also vicariously for others.

68. Cf. *tada drashtuh svarupe avasthanam*, Yogasutra 1.3. Cf. Brih. Up. 2.4.14, where Yajnavalkya describes Atman, called there Vijñatri, in his true and absolute state, in which there is no objectivity whatsoever.

69. Mundaka Up. 1.1.3 (Cf. also Chandogya Up. 6.1.2.3).
70. The Buddha is reported to have recovered the memories of eighty-four past world-periods, an immense stretch of time almost impossible of comprehension.
71. Cf. Chandogya Up. 7.26.2: *ahara-shuddhau sattva-shuddhih; sattva-shuddhau dhruva smritih; smriti-lambhe sarva-granthinam vipramokshah.*
72. Cf. Taittiriya Up. 2.1; so *'shnute sarvan kaman saha brahmana.*
73. This is the real meaning and explanation of certain passages which have been erroneously interpreted as sanctioning unbridled license on the part of one who is freed. On the transcending of ethical distinctions see Brih. Up. 4.3.22; Chandogya Up. 4.14.3; Mundaka Up. 3.1.3; Prashna Up. 5.5. The full signifcance of such passages will be understood by comparison with the saying of St. Augustine, "Love God and do what you will."
74. Such remnants of moral and spiritual debts are technically called Prarabdha Karma, Karma that has already begun its operation. It is only one of three classes into which Karma was analyzed in later times, but, no doubt, in accordance with principles underlying the idea of Karma as treated in the Vedic texts. The three classes of Karma are:

1. The Karma which is being produced by thought or action at any particular time and will subsequently come to fruition (*kriyamana*). Of this newly created Karma only a small portion can find its ultimation in that same

lifetime; the major portion remains latent as a cause of events and character in a subsequent life.

2. The Karma which, not having found an opportunity of bring about the appropriate results during the incarnation in which it was produced, has gone on accumulating from ages past and is waiting for a suitable opportunity to show itself in results (*samcita*).

3. The Karma selected out of this accumulated heap in such a manner that the selected portions can produce results without them being mutually nullifying (*prarabdha*).

It is this Prarabdha Karma which determines the present incarnation of a soul with all its possibilities, both subjectively in regard to one's character and capacities and objectively in regard to situation and environment. Prarabdha Karma has to be self-consistent, as otherwise it cannot work. For instance, it cannot be such that it will make one both blind and full-visioned from birth or both poor and wealthy throughout life.

Prarabdha Karma is, moreover, obligation which one must face and endure, or enjoy as the case may be. It is not possible to escape it, and often it is not morally right to attempt to shirk it. It is not right to shirk it because by so doing a person strengthens the feeling of separateness, which, in other words, is selfishness and leads away from the ultimate goal of life, namely the realization of oneness. It will be observed that one never shirks duty except for selfish reasons— fear, idleness, and the like. Hence a yogi does not run away from Prarabdha Karma, that is, duties and obligations of life, even when it is possible to do so, but performs them to the uttermost, even unto death. While Prarabdha must be faced, the accumulated Karma, which is held together by the unconscious ego, is destroyed as soon as this ego is destroyed, on the realization of oneness, and accumulated Karma, which readily constituted one's individuality, is seen in positive experience as something other than one's real Self, now realized as one with the Self of all.

75. What the measure of the joy and love (*ananda*) of one who is freed may be has been described in two striking passages in the Upanishads. The most perfect and ideal state of bliss for a human being, as human, is taken as the unit. We are then told how the bliss of the next stage of spiritual advancement or next higher state of superhuman existence is a hundred times the unit of the most perfect human bliss; and how the bliss of the third stage is a hundred times that of the second, and so on; till we come to a measure of bliss which, as expressed in an arithmetical figure, is really inconceivable. And this inconceivably and immeasurably great bliss is finally held up as the bliss of Brahman and of the liberated one who has realized oneness with Brahman. See Brih. Up. 4.3.33; Taittiriya Up. 2.8.

76. Cf. Viveka-cudamani.

77. With regard to death by an act of the will, see page 58 and note 36.

78. Cf. Luke 20.36. It is noteworthy that the more typical way of expressing the idea of reincarnation in the older texts is not "rebirth" but "redeath" (*punarmrityu*). And the perfected

one "overcomes repeated death" (*apa punarm-rityum jayati*, Brih. Up. 1.2.7). In view of this fact the expression used in Luke 20.36, "neither can they die any more," is very striking indeed.

79. Cf. Prashna Up. 4.10: *sa sarvajñah, sarvo bhavati,* and many other passages in praise of the one finally freed.

Cf. also Isha Upanishad 8, which, it may be noted, refers to the seer who has the oneness with all, mentioned in the two immediately preceding Mantras.

It may be noted here that the Christian doctrine of Christ "judging the quick and the dead" seems hardly different from the Vedic idea of the freed one who has been dispensing things according to their rightness (*yathatathyato 'rthan vyadadhac chashvatibhyah samabhyah,* Isha Up. 8).

80. Vikramorvashiyam 1.1.

81. That is, in the Upanishads.

82. This word, *rodasi,* from *rud,* "to roar, cry," is of the same meaning as the word *krandasi* occurring in RV. 2.12.8; 6.25.4; 10.121.6.

83. See above, pages 52-53.

84. The term *bhakti* is defined as *paranuraktir Ishvare,* "all-surpassing, supreme love for the Lord."

85. Absolute Freedom, the state of abiding Being, unconditioned Awareness, and unmixed Joy and Love.

Appendix

A. *On Vivarta, the Athanasian Creed, and the Christian View of Immanence*

The writer of the foregoing pages has been told by several persons that the idea that the one ultimate Divine Being apparently divides and appears in countless forms as the universe, yet without undergoing any change whatsoever (page 23 above), is to them strange and difficult of comprehension. This conception of the universal process, technically called *vivarta*, is, however, not entirely foreign to Christianity.

The Athanasian Creed, when it speaks of the one God becoming Three Persons "without dividing the substances," is undoubtedly expressing a similar idea, except that the conception of God entertained by the average Christian of ancient and modern times is that of an extracosmic entity and quite "naïve and anthropomorphic." This was the case, according to Professor McGiffert, even with Jesus (*The God of the Early Christians,* New York, 1924, page 4). It is, however, a view which the present writer does not believe to be correct, even though the synoptic Gospels—on which Professor McGiffert relies for his statement, and which are now recognized to be later than the letters of Paul and written by Jews who were naturally predisposed to see their own ancestral conceptions in the teachings of Jesus—may have represented Jesus as holding such an idea. On the contrary, the conception of the Deity held by Jesus was really that of a Being who is certainly immanent in every living soul, in every thing and being, so that Jesus could proclaim: "Behold, the kingdom of God is within you" (Luke 17.21), putting into the phrase "kingdom of God" a new meaning totally at variance with any conception the Hebrews might have had about their own theocratic "kingdom." That he also believed in the transcendent aspect of the Deity is obvious from the fact that average Christians, basing their belief on the teachings of Jesus, regard God as something away from this world, somewhere in the upper heavens, where, they further believe, Jesus himself went up in his physical body when he "rose from the dead," as the saying goes. That this is only a naive, popular way of regarding the idea of transcendence can hardly be doubted.

In any case, the Vedic doctrine of *vivarta* and immanence should not be considered strange now, in view of the epoch-making statement, in the encyclical accompanying the resolution of the Lambeth Conference of 1930, saying: "Scientific thinking and discovery seems to be giving us back the sense of reverence and awe before the Creator, *Who is not only the cause and ground of the universe, but is always everywhere and active within it.*" (The italics are the present writer's.)

This is exactly the view which the Vedic Indians and those incorporated in their communities have held from time immemorial. Only it should be added that, in the Vedic view, the Divine Being is not only immanent in the universe as the only ground, the only substance, and the ceaseless controller of all that is—there being no other substance, controller, or abiding reality whatsoever—but is also, at the same time and forever, a transcendent Being, beyond and above all relation to the universe. The Divine Being is, in other words, at once both the Transcendent and the Immanent Deity, "without dividing the substance."

B. *On the Term "Dullness"*

Professor E. Washburn Hopkins, who has placed the writer under a deep debt of obligation by his careful and sympathetic consideration of the foregoing pages, has raised only one serious objection, as follows:

"I should like to suggest that *avarana* (on page 102) is a *mayashakti* of an active nature just like *vikshepa* in being an activity (antithetic to *vikshepa*), and as you render *vikshepa* quite rightly by 'distraction,' so *avarana* is not the passive negative 'dullness' itself, but the cause of the dullness, and it is so because it is literally the 'closure' or 'immurement,' that is, an active power, suppressing and so making the mind dull, rather than the dullness itself; 'shutting up' or 'bolting in' the mind (*avarana* actually means a 'bolt' as well as the more common activity of 'enclosing'). I do not know whether this will appeal to you, but that is the way it seems to me, especially as *avarana* and *vikshepa* are defined as *shaktidvayam* (two antithetic powers) and dullness results from *avarana*, just as a lack of concentration does from *vikshepa*."

The writer fully agrees with Professor Hopkins and accepts this kindly criticism. He believed, however, that from what was said about the true nature of the universal process as being the manifestation of a living, conscious, and active Energy (*shakti*), starting with the tremendous act of negating and suppressing the abiding Being—an act which produces the first notion of Universal Nothingness—it would be understood by readers that even "dullness," like sleep, though apparently passive, was really due to the operation of an active energy. The writer is, however, grateful to Professor Hopkins for drawing attention to what evidently might easily be misunderstood and for him giving this opportunity of clearing the matter up.

Index

149

Index

Index

Related Quest Titles

Man, God, and the Universe, I. K. Taimni

Mother of the Universe, Lex Hixon